★ THIBAUD VILLANOVA ★

TOP SECRET

GASTRONO GEEK

RECIPES TO DIE FOR

★ PHOTOGRAPHY ★
Nicolas **LOBBESTAËL**

★ STYLING ★
Séverine **AUGÉ**

INSIGHT
EDITIONS

SAN RAFAEL · LOS ANGELES · LONDON

SUSPECT?

INVESTIGATION REPORT

THE COOKBOOK YOU HOLD IN YOUR HANDS IS DEDICATED TO ALL THE SPECIAL INVESTIGATORS, FAMOUS DETECTIVES, AND BEAT COPS WHO ALWAYS HAVE TIME FOR A SNACK BEFORE HUNTING DOWN THE MOST NEFARIOUS MURDERERS AND CRIMINALS!

If you're not familiar with my work, you should know that, since 2014, I've been creating recipes inspired by the most popular movies, TV series, manga, fantasy novels, and video games. I love digging into these imaginary worlds to find out what our favorite heroes like to eat or to sometimes ponder what they might have eaten. I conduct a thorough investigation: I reread the novels, rewatch the films and episodes, and play through the games again to refresh my memories of the details. After I create a recipe, I meticulously design a themed setting for the dish (and I hide Easter eggs among the utensils and ingredients). For each recipe, my goal is simply to make food that invites the reader to linger a little longer in a familiar universe. Like a detective, I embark on a carefully thought-out process. Every recipe that appears in this book is designed not only to transport you and feed your imagination, but also to help you easily cook delicious food!

Like many of you, I imagine, I've been fascinated by detectives and mystery novels since I was a kid. I inherited this fascination from my mother, who first turned me on to reading. I can still picture her well-stocked library, much of it devoted to mysteries. I remember the first ones I read, from *Alfred Hitchcock and the Three Investigators* (actually written by Robert Arthur Jr.) to the classics by Sir Arthur Conan Doyle. I think I read the *Arsène Lupin* books around the same time I discovered Sherlock Holmes.

INVESTIGATION REPORT

After falling in love with the genre as a young reader, I devoured the works of Agatha Christie, becoming fast friends with her protagonists, Hercule Poirot and Jane Marple. At the same time, I was developing an appetite for crime and action movies; I watched all the movies and shows from the 1980s, along with 1970s TV series that were still getting air time. I saw *Bullit,* of course, along with *The Streets of San Francisco*; *Starsky & Hutch*; *Columbo*; *Murder, She Wrote*; and *Poirot*, the series starring David Suchet (the true face of the Belgian detective, obviously!). Even today, I'll never say no to an episode of *Castle* or a new version of *Murder on the Orient Express*.

Now that we've set the scene, let's dive into this collection of recipes inspired, eaten, and cooked by the biggest names in the genre: characters from Japan, like Detective Conan; occult detectives, like Hellboy and John Constantine; heroes of classic TV series, like Jessica Fletcher, Remington Steele, and Magnum, P.I.; and cops working every beat, from Harry Bosch in Los Angeles to Maigret in France. Together we'll share childhood memories with Miss Marple at Bertram's Hotel, and we'll try some dishes drawn from the adventures of Hercule Poirot, including a Christmas pudding! A few pages pay homage to some fascinating characters who have captured my imagination despite being on the wrong side of the law.

I hope you have as much fun exploring this part of my world as I did writing the recipes. Enjoy the book—and your dinner, too!

May the Fork be with you, always.

THIBAUD VILLANOVA
GASTRONOGEEK

CONTENTS

RISE AND CRIME

BREAKFAST

THE HORS-D'OEUVRE AFFAIR

APPETIZERS

SMASH AND GRAB

FAST FOOD

THE POT THICKENS

COMFORT FOOD

THE POT THICKENS

JUST DESSERTS

HIGH-PROOF SOLUTIONS

RISE
AND CRIME

BREAKFAST

People often say that breakfast is the most important meal of the day, the one that fuels your body for the challenges ahead. I'm not sure that's true. Personally, I always start my day with a big cup of black coffee, but luckily for this book, the likes of Hellboy and Miss Marple have other ideas.

BREAKFAST WITH PERNILLA

SALMON SMØRREBRØD WITH SCRAMBLED EGGS, CHEESE, AND CUCUMBER

DIFFICULTY	EASY
PREP TIME	15 MINUTES
COOK TIME	15 MINUTES
YIELD	4 SERVINGS

CASE NOTES: *You're never there for your daughter. Luckily for you, she doesn't hold grudges, and she travels across the country to join you in Hedestad, where you're conducting your investigation. You finally get a minute to talk over a cup of coffee and a good breakfast. Good thing, too, because her familiarity with the Book of Leviticus offers the fresh perspective that jump-starts your stalled investigation. You're ready to get back to the case—after one last smørrebrød!*

INGREDIENTS

4 thick slices of Nordic bread or rye bread

½ cucumber

8 tablespoons unsalted butter

4 fillets organic salmon or trout

Juice of 1 lemon

10 eggs

A few chives

Flaky sea salt, for sprinkling

4 generous slices Herrgårdsost or Emmental cheese

Handful of baby spinach

A few stems dill

Pickled red onion or pickled beets, for garnishing

★ Evenly spread ½ tablespoon of the butter over each slice of bread.

★ Slice the cucumber into rounds.

★ Melt 1 tablespoon of the butter in a frying pan. Lightly salt the fish fillets; then cook the fillets over medium heat for 4 to 5 minutes on each side until they are golden brown and cooked through. Deglaze with the lemon juice, and set aside.

★ Break the eggs into a saucepan. Cube the remaining 5 tablespoons of butter, and add it to the eggs. Finely chop the chives, and add them to the saucepan.

★ Place the saucepan over medium heat, and stir with a wooden spatula. Stirring constantly, melt the butter and cook the eggs, with the saucepan alternately on and off the heat. This will result in scrambled eggs that are soft and custardy—never dry. When the eggs are cooked, transfer them to a bowl, sprinkle with flaky sea salt, and set aside. (It is best to wait to salt until you are done cooking the eggs, or else they will be runny.)

★ To assemble the smørrebrød, place a slice of cheese on each piece of buttered bread. Top with a few cucumber rounds, followed by a few leaves of baby spinach, the fried fish, and then a few spoonfuls of scrambled eggs. Garnish with dill and pickled onions or beets for flavor, texture, and color.

BREAKFAST AT BERTRAM'S HOTEL

FRIED EGGS, BACON, AND SCONES WITH JAM

DIFFICULTY	EASY
PREP TIME	15 MINUTES
COOK TIME	30 MINUTES
YIELD	4 SERVINGS

CASE NOTES: *Bertram's Hotel in London is probably Miss Marple's favorite vacation haunt. She loves the hotel's old-school charm, the childhood memories it brings back, and, of course, its fabulous English breakfasts! After all, why not savor a scone or two before starting a new investigation into the latest mysterious murder?*

INGREDIENTS

Vanilla Scones

¾ cup plus 2 tablespoons milk

1 vanilla bean

4 tablespoons unsalted butter, at room temperature

2 cups flour, sifted

¼ cup sugar

2 teaspoons baking powder

Pinch of salt

1 egg yolk, beaten

Berry jam, for spreading on scones

8 thick slices bacon or porchetta

8 large eggs

4 tablespoons butter or vegetable oil

Salt and pepper

Aleppo pepper

★ Preheat the oven to 350°F.

★ To make the scones, first infuse the milk with vanilla: Pour the milk into a saucepan, and bring it to a gentle boil. While the milk is warming, use the tip of a paring knife to split open the vanilla bean lengthwise. Scrape out the seeds, and add both the seeds and the pod to the milk. Continue to cook at a gentle boil for about 10 minutes; then remove the vanilla pod from the saucepan, turn off the heat, and set aside the vanilla-infused milk.

★ Place the butter in a large bowl. Beat with a silicone spatula until softened; then add the flour, sugar, baking powder, and salt. Pour in the vanilla-infused milk, and stir until the mixture forms a dough.

★ Form the dough into a ball. Place the dough between two pieces of parchment paper, and form it into a disc just over 1 inch thick. Use a cookie cutter to cut out rounds.

★ Arrange the dough rounds on a baking sheet lined with parchment paper. Brush the egg yolk over the scones, and bake them for 15 minutes or until golden brown. Halve the scones, and spread with blueberry jam. Set aside.

★ Arrange the slices of bacon in a cold frying pan, and begin to cook over medium heat. Starting with a cold pan allows the bacon to cook in its own fat and brown nicely. Cook the bacon for 4 to 5 minutes, turning halfway. Remove the bacon from the pan, and set it on a paper towel.

★ Add 1 tablespoon of the vegetable oil or butter to a frying pan, and warm the pan over medium heat. When the pan is very hot, break 2 eggs into it. Fry the eggs until the yolk is cooked to your taste. After they are cooked, season the eggs with a pinch of salt, black pepper, and Aleppo pepper. Repeat for the remaining eggs, adding a tablespoon of butter for every 2 eggs.

★ To plate, for each guest, prepare a plate of 2 fried eggs, 2 slices of bacon, and some scones with berry jam. Serve with freshly pressed orange juice and tea with lemon.

DEMON PANCAKES

PANCAKES WITH CHEDDAR, BACON, AND BARBECUE SAUCE

DIFFICULTY	EASY
PREP TIME	15 MINUTES
COOK TIME	30 MINUTES
YIELD	4 SERVINGS

CASE NOTES: *In 1947, Hellboy was just a kid. Gen. Norton Ricker served the picky hellspawn his first pancakes, and it was love at first bite.*

INGREDIENTS

Pancakes

1½ cups milk

5 tablespoons butter, plus 1 pat for cooking

2½ cups flour

2 teaspoons baking powder

1 teaspoon salt

⅛ cup sugar

3 eggs

1 teaspoon vanilla extract

3½ ounces cheddar cheese, in small cubes

1 teaspoon dried thyme

Marinated Bacon

1 tablespoon tomato paste

1 teaspoon Worcestershire sauce

1 tablespoon olive oil

1 teaspoon ketchup, homemade (see page 116) or organic store bought

1 teaspoon maple syrup

½ teaspoon Tabasco® sauce

1 tablespoon dark rum

10 slices bacon

Identification: BACON

Identification: PANCAKES

DEMON PANCAKES

CASE FILE, PAGE 2

METHOD

★ To prepare the bacon: Position the oven rack directly underneath the broiler, and preheat the oven to 425°F. Add all the ingredients for the marinade to a mixing bowl, and stir well. Coat the bacon slices with the marinade, and arrange them on a baking sheet lined with parchment paper. Bake for 5 minutes; then flip and bake for an additional 1 to 2 minutes. Remove the bacon from the oven, and set aside.

★ To make the pancake batter: Pour the milk into a saucepan, add the 5 tablespoons of butter, and warm over medium heat until the butter is completely melted. Set aside. Add the flour, baking powder, salt, and sugar to a mixing bowl. Form a well, and break the eggs into it. Add the vanilla. Whisk the eggs into the dry ingredients. While continuing to whisk, slowly pour in the milk and melted butter mixture. Finally, stir in the cheddar and thyme.

★ Melt a pat of butter in a small frying pan over medium heat. When the butter starts to sizzle, pour a ladle of batter into the pan, and swirl to spread it out evenly. Cook the pancake until small bubbles form on its surface, then flip. Repeat for each pancake until you have used all the batter.

★ Serve the pancakes piping hot with the bacon. If you really want to channel Hellboy, feel free to enjoy your breakfast with a cold beer!

THE HORS-D'OEUVRE AFFAIR

APPETIZERS

All good plans start with an introduction.

The same is true for a meal. The appetizer sets the tone for what will follow, tantalizing your tastebuds and stirring up memories that you have locked away. A bowl of French onion soup, for example, might remind you of the charming bistro you stumbled across years ago in France; a lobster roll can transport you straight to Cabot Cove, Maine; and a few oysters with vinaigrette savored to the sounds of jazz will conjure up the decadence of old Paris, the glittering city whose light is, on occasion, dimmed by a horrible crime . . .

CAFÉ RÉPLIQUE
FRENCH ONION SOUP

CHEESE GRATINÉE WITH ONION AND COGNAC BROTH

DIFFICULTY	EASY
PREP TIME	30 MINUTES
COOK TIME	30 MINUTES
YIELD	4 SERVINGS

CASE NOTES: *What a lark—meeting up with an old friend to recall the times you spent together in Paris when you used to pose for famous painters! Why not enjoy some classic French cuisine while you're at it, and head to Café Réplique for a hot bowl of French onion soup?*

INGREDIENTS

1 pound yellow onions

6 tablespoons unsalted butter

Salt and pepper

5 tablespoons flour

8 cups chicken, vegetable, or beef broth, either homemade (see page 115) or store bought

½ cup cognac

½ baguette, stale

14 ounces Gruyère cheese

★ First, peel and thinly slice the onions.

★ Cut the butter into large pieces, and add them to a Dutch oven. Melt the butter over medium heat; then add the sliced onions. Season sparingly with salt and pepper, and cook until the onions turn golden brown. Sprinkle in the flour, and stir well with a wooden spatula to mix.

★ Pour in the broth, and bring to a gentle boil. Cook for 30 to 35 minutes, stirring regularly. At the very end of cooking, add the cognac and set aside over very low heat.

★ Position the oven rack directly underneath the broiler, and preheat the oven to 425°F. Cut the baguette into ½-inch thick slices. Grate half the cheese, and cut the remainder into thin strips.

★ Assemble the individual bowls of soup: In the bottom of each soup bowl, place 1 slice of bread and then a few strips of Gruyère. Add another layer of bread and cheese, and finish with a slice of bread. Cover with caramelized onions and broth, sprinkle with grated Gruyère, and broil in the oven for 2 minutes.

★ Enjoy piping hot!

CABOT COVE LOBSTER ROLLS

LOBSTER SALAD WITH GREEN ONIONS ON SANDWICH ROLLS

DIFFICULTY	MEDIUM
PREP TIME	15 MINUTES
COOK TIME	20 MINUTES
YIELD	4 SERVINGS

CASE NOTES: *It's not unusual for Seth to find Jessica Fletcher in the kitchen, baking a cake or cooking lobster. Follow this recipe, and you'll be on your way to a Maine staple, just like Jessica might have made herself. Home-made or ordered at the Leg & Claw, no doubt lobster is a Cabot Cove delight!*

INGREDIENTS

Sandwiches

2 live lobsters, about 1 pound each (or the meat of 2 Maine lobsters)

Sea salt, for sprinkling

6 tablespoons unsalted butter

4 sandwich rolls

A few chives

Green Onion Mayonnaise

½ bunch fresh green onions

1 stem fresh tarragon

1 tablespoon capers

2 egg yolks

2 tablespoons spicy mustard

1 cup sunflower oil

1 tablespoon ketchup, homemade (see page 116) or store bought

1 teaspoon gin

Juice of 1 lemon

Salt and freshly ground pepper

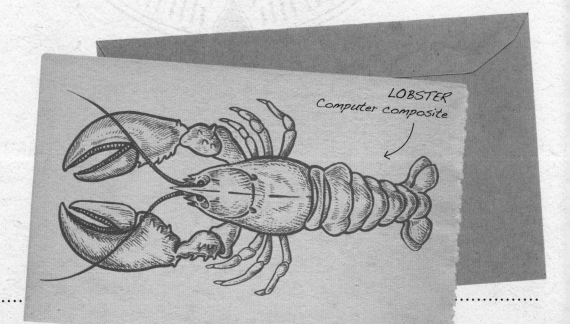

LOBSTER
Computer composite

CABOT COVE
LOBSTER ROLLS

CASE FILE, PAGE 2

METHOD

★ You can always ask your fishmonger to prepare them for you, but if you prefer to tackle them yourself, begin by preparing the lobsters: Fill a large Dutch oven two-thirds full with water and bring to a boil, sprinkling generously with sea salt (about 1 tablespoon of salt for every 4 cups of water). Set each lobster on a cutting board, in turn. Place the point of a chef's knife at the cross mark on the shell and plunge the knife down in a single motion, splitting the head in half. This will kill the lobster quickly and painlessly.

★ Drop the lobsters into the boiling water, cover, and cook for 12 to 15 minutes from the time the water returns to a boil. Drain the lobsters, and let cool in a strainer; set aside.

★ To make the mayonnaise: Rinse and finely chop the green onions and tarragon leaves. Chop the capers. Add the egg yolks to a mixing bowl, and whisk in the mustard; drizzle in the sunflower oil while continuing to whisk. Add the ketchup, gin, and lemon juice. Season with salt and freshly ground pepper. Finally, stir in the green onions, tarragon, and capers; set aside.

★ Shell the lobsters, and cut the meat into generous pieces. Add the lobster meat to the mayonnaise, and set aside.

★ Melt the butter in a frying pan over low heat, and brown the sandwich rolls on all sides. Open each roll, and fill with lobster salad. Finely chop the chives, and sprinkle over the lobster meat.

Enjoy!

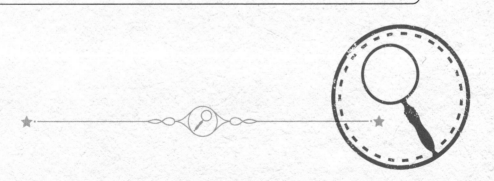

TERRASSON'S ANCHOVIES

HERB-MARINATED ANCHOVIES ON TOAST

DIFFICULTY	EASY
PREP TIME	15 MINUTES
RESTING TIME	14 HOURS
COOK TIME	5 MINUTES
YIELD	4 SERVINGS

CASE NOTES: *Terrasson is a giant of a man and a member of a crack team of police motorcycle officers. His strength is equaled only by his courage—which, in turn, is equaled only by his appetite for life and for little hors d'oeuvre picnics! Here's a quick recipe for a small plate featuring freshly caught anchovies.*

INGREDIENTS

14 ounces fresh anchovies

⅔ cup white vinegar

⅓ cup lemon juice

1 tablespoon flaky sea salt

Ground Aleppo pepper, for sprinkling

½ bunch flat-leaf parsley

2 cloves garlic

½ cup olive oil

A few slices of rustic bread

1 tomato

★ Clean the anchovies: Cut off their heads and remove their guts by slitting the fish from the base of the head to the tail. Rinse in fresh water.

★ Place the anchovies in a mixing bowl. Pour the vinegar, lemon juice, and salt over the fish to cover. Cover tightly with plastic wrap, and refrigerate for about 2 hours.

★ Drain the anchovies, and arrange them in a dish. Sprinkle with Aleppo pepper. Chop the parsley and 1 garlic clove, and add it to the anchovies. Drizzle generously with most of the olive oil. Cover tightly with plastic wrap again, and refrigerate for 12 hours.

★ Just before serving, brush the bread slices with the remaining olive oil. Heat a frying pan over high heat, and toast the bread on both sides. Halve the remaining garlic clove and tomato, and then rub each slice of toast with garlic and tomato.

★ Serve the marinated anchovies over the garlic and tomato toast.

LA TOUR D'IVOIRE OYSTERS

OYSTERS WITH VINAIGRETTE TRIO

DIFFICULTY	EASY
PREP TIME	15 MINUTES
YIELD	4 SERVINGS

CASE NOTES: *You had no clue what would befall your old friend Pierre de Fabrègues when you heard his message on the answering machine. You could smell trouble in the kitchen at his restaurant, La Tour d'Ivoire, though, and you knew you were going to have to get your hands dirty. Maybe you can take a break from grilling the kitchen boys long enough to eat a few oysters.*

INGREDIENTS

Classic Mignonette

1 shallot

2 tablespoons raspberry vinegar

Salt and pepper

Umami Vinaigrette

½-inch piece fresh ginger

2 tablespoons soy sauce

1 tablespoon mirin

Italian Vinaigrette

A few leaves of fresh basil

A handful of pine nuts

2 tablespoons red wine vinegar

1 tablespoon olive oil

12 medium (size 3) fresh oysters

Large quantity of crushed ice

★ Prepare the trio of vinaigrettes.

★ For the classic mignonette, peel and finely chop the shallot. Add the shallot to a small mixing bowl; then add the raspberry vinegar, salt, and pepper. Mix well, and set aside.

★ For the umami vinaigrette, peel and finely chop the ginger. Add the ginger to a small bowl, along with the soy sauce and mirin. Stir well, and set aside.

★ For the Italian vinaigrette, roll the basil leaves together into a tight cylinder, and slice thinly. Crush the pine nuts. Add the basil and pine nuts to a small bowl, and pour in the vinegar and olive oil. Mix well, and set aside.

★ Carefully open the oysters, and arrange them on a bed of crushed ice. Serve with the flavored vinaigrettes and a glass of champagne for each guest. *Bon appétit!*

ASPARAGUS VICHYSSOISE

CHILLED ASPARAGUS SOUP

DIFFICULTY	EASY
PREP TIME	10 MINUTES
RESTING TIME	1 HOUR
COOK TIME	35 MINUTES
YIELD	4 SERVINGS

CASE NOTES: *Being Professor Layton's adopted daughter comes with a certain set of expectations: You should be able to solve any riddle, no matter what. That's true even when it involves putting together the perfect menu and mastering a mountain of new recipes—including this classic French soup!*

INGREDIENTS

7 ounces asparagus

1 bunch chives

7 ounces yellow potatoes

3 tablespoons unsalted butter

1 teaspoon salt

1 cup heavy cream

Black pepper

★ Wash the asparagus stalks, and chop them into small pieces of equal size. Finely chop the chives, and set aside. Peel the potatoes, and cut them into ⅛-inch cubes.

★ In a saucepan, melt the butter over low heat; then add the asparagus. Sweat the asparagus in the butter for 4 minutes, and then add the potato cubes. Stir to combine, and add cold water to cover. Season with salt, and cook over medium heat for 30 minutes.

★ Remove the saucepan from the heat. Use an immersion blender to blend the contents of the saucepan; then let cool to room temperature.

★ Add the heavy cream to the saucepan, and mix well. Pour the resulting soup through a fine strainer, and refrigerate for at least 1 hour.

★ Serve this soup chilled, sprinkled with black pepper and chopped chives.

SMASH
AND GRAB

FAST FOOD

When you're on a stakeout or in hot pursuit, you don't always have time to sit down to a full meal. Sometimes it's all you can do to grab a quick bite on the go. Everyone has a favorite go-to spot, but even then, you might just have to drop your burger or hot dog to nab the crooks before they can hold up the joint!

Maybe you'd better just pack your own lunch . . . and cross your fingers that no one poisons your sandwich.

NEW YORK JOE'S PIZZA

PEPPERONI-CHEDDAR PIZZA

DIFFICULTY	MEDIUM
PREP TIME	20 MINUTES
RESTING TIME	12 HOURS
COOK TIME	12 TO 15 MINUTES
YIELD	4 SERVINGS

CASE NOTES: *To most people, New York is a big, shiny, juicy apple. But it takes more than sparkle to impress an old hand like Mike Hammer. He knows that this apple is riddled with worms and that its innards smell of blood, sweat, and crime. It's easy to lose your appetite pacing the streets of a city like that—unless you have a strong stomach and a craving for a great slice of pizza. Whaddya say, Mike?*

INGREDIENTS

Homemade Pizza Dough

½ cup water, at room temperature

¾ teaspoon active dry yeast

1 teaspoon olive oil,
plus more for resting the dough

1¼ cup flour,
plus more for resting the dough

½ teaspoon table salt

Toppings

½ cup tomato sauce

5 ounces mozzarella cheese, sliced

2 ounces cheddar cheese, shredded

2½ ounces pepperoni, sliced

★ The night before, make the pizza dough: Pour the water, yeast, and teaspoon of olive oil into a mixing bowl. Use a whisk or fork to stir the mixture vigorously, then let it rest for 10 minutes.

★ In a separate mixing bowl, stir together 1¼ cup flour and the salt, then add the mixed wet ingredients. Continue to mix with your fingers for about 5 minutes until the dough forms a ball. Let rest for 10 minutes.

★ Dust your work surface with the additional flour, and turn out the dough to knead it for another 3 to 4 minutes. Oil and flour a mixing bowl, place the ball of dough in it, and cover the bowl with plastic wrap. Leave the mixing bowl in the refrigerator for at least 12 hours while the dough doubles in volume.

★ When you're ready to bake the pizza the next day, preheat the oven to 425°F. Form the pizza dough into a thin round on a baking sheet lined with parchment paper. Spread the tomato sauce over the dough. Cover the entire pizza with slices of mozzarella and shredded cheddar cheese. Top the pizza with pepperoni slices; then bake for 12 to 15 minutes.

★ Enjoy piping hot!

ELINOR CARLISLE'S SANDWICHES

SANDWICHES WITH SALMON TWO WAYS AND CRAB & SHRIMP SALAD

DIFFICULTY	EASY
PREP TIME	10 MINUTES
COOK TIME	10 MINUTES
YIELD	4 SERVINGS

CASE NOTES: *Hercule Poirot's brain is not the only thing about him that's sharp: So is his sense of taste. It comes in handy for detecting poison and dangerous substances, not to mention surviving British cuisine and "the ignorance of the English palate." There's no doubt that Elinor Carlisle's sandwiches will remain etched in his memory. Follow this recipe, and you'll soon be sitting down to a plate of sandwiches worthy of the great Hercule Poirot!*

INGREDIENTS

16 slices sandwich bread

Salmon Filling	Crab and Shrimp Salad
A few chives	6 cooked shrimp
½ bunch fresh dill	1 shallot
Olive oil, for brushing	A few chives
1 fillet salmon	Drizzle of olive oil
Pinch of salt	Pinch of pepper
1 slice smoked salmon	2 tablespoons cream cheese
2 tablespoons cream cheese	2 drops Tabasco® sauce
Pinch of salt and pepper	
Juice of 1 lemon	

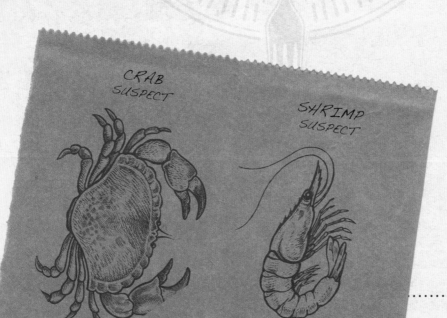

CRAB SUSPECT

SHRIMP SUSPECT

ELINOR CARLISLE'S SANDWICHES

CASE FILE, PAGE 2

★ To make the salmon filling: Finely chop the chives and dill. Pour the olive oil into a frying pan over medium heat. Place the salmon fillet in the hot pan, skin side down. Salt lightly, and sauté for 5 to 6 minutes or until cooked through. Remove the salmon from the pan, set it on a paper towel, and use a fork to flake it into pieces.

★ Position the oven rack directly underneath the broiler, and pre-heat the oven to 400°F.

★ Cube the smoked salmon, and add both the smoked salmon pieces and the flaked salmon to a food processor. Add the cream cheese, salt and pepper, lemon juice, dill, and chives. Process until creamy; set aside.

★ To make the crab and shrimp salad: Peel and chop the shrimp; set aside. Peel and finely chop the shallot. Finely chop the chives. Add all the ingredients to the food processor. Process until creamy.

★ Cut the crusts off the bread. Use a brush to lightly coat the bread with olive oil; then toast for 2 minutes (or until browned) under the broiler.

★ Spread 4 slices of bread with a generous layer of salmon filling, and top each with another slice of bread. Repeat the process for the crab and shrimp salad.

★ Cut each sandwich in half diagonally, and serve.

BOO KOO'S BURGER

1930s-STYLE DOUBLE-DECKER BURGER

DIFFICULTY	EASY
PREP TIME	10 MINUTES
COOK TIME	5 MINUTES
YIELD	4 SERVINGS

CASE NOTES: *Perry Mason hasn't always been the defense attorney we know from the series. He began his career in Los Angeles as a private investigator in the 1930s and lived from case to case. He and his friend Pete Strickland, another private detective, had many a working meeting over dinner at Boo Koo Burger Stand.*

INGREDIENTS

⅛ bunch fresh parsley

1 red onion

1 teaspoon salt, plus more for seasoning

2 to 3 tablespoons flour

Oil for frying

12½ ounces ground beef

1 teaspoon cumin

1 teaspoon paprika

1 teaspoon pepper

Sunflower oil, for greasing the pan

Mustard, homemade (see page 116) or store bought

4 hamburger buns, homemade (see page 114) or store bought

4 large leaves lettuce

Homemade sweet and sour pickles (see page 117)

★ Chop the parsley and set aside. Slice the onion into thick rings; salt lightly and set in the flour, then set aside.

★ Pour enough oil into a fryer or saucepan to cover the bottom, and heat to a temperature of 320°F. Drop the breaded red onion slices into the hot oil, and cook for 1 to 2 minutes. Remove the fried onion from the oil, and set aside on a paper towel.

★ Add the ground beef to a mixing bowl, along with the spices, 1 teaspoon salt, and pepper. Mix thoroughly, and then form the meat into 8 balls of equal size. Flatten each ball between 2 sheets of parchment paper.

★ Heat a cast iron frying pan with a drizzle of sunflower oil, or set a grill over high heat. Sear the patties for 1 minute on each side; then reduce the heat to medium, and continue cooking for 4 minutes until the meat is cooked through. Set aside the patties on a piece of parchment paper and cover while you assemble the burgers.

★ To assemble the burgers: Spread homemade mustard on the inside of both halves of the bun. Top one side with a leaf of lettuce, slices of homemade pickles, one patty, some fried onion rings, and then another patty; cover with the other half of the bun. Repeat the process for all 4 burgers. Wrap tightly in greaseproof paper.

★ Enjoy the burgers hot, then get back to tracking down the bad guys!

JUMBO STAKEOUT
HOT DOG

BEEF FRANKS WITH HOMEMADE BUNS AND RELISH

DIFFICULTY	MEDIUM
PREP TIME	15 MINUTES
RESTING TIME	1 HOUR
COOK TIME	15 TO 20 MINUTES
YIELD	4 SERVINGS

CASE NOTES: *You've been having a bite to eat, maybe a hot dog or two, when you suddenly notice a beige sedan parked in front of the bank, motor running. Better call HQ, take one last bite of your jumbo dog, and draw your .44! Just don't let Inspector Callahan catch you putting ketchup on your hot dog.*

INGREDIENTS

Hot Dog Buns

2¼ cups cake flour, plus more for the work surface

1 teaspoon salt

1 teaspoon sugar

1 packet (¾ ounce) active dry yeast

Scant ½ cup milk

2 eggs plus 1 yolk for glazing

1½ tablespoons unsalted butter, softened

4 beef franks

4 tablespoons homemade relish (see page 117)

Yellow mustard, for garnishing

Homemade ketchup (see page 116), for garnishing (if you dare)

★ To make the buns: Add the flour, salt, and sugar to the bowl of a stand mixer. Add the yeast to the bowl, taking care not to let it touch the salt yet. Add the milk and whole eggs. Use a dough hook to knead for 5 minutes on medium speed. The resulting dough should be sticky and stretchy. Add the butter, and knead for an additional 3 minutes to combine.

★ With the help of a bowl scraper or spatula, move the dough to a mixing bowl. Cover with a damp cloth, and let rise for 30 minutes.

★ Dust your work surface with a little flour, and place the ball of dough on it. Punch down the dough to deflate it, and then knead again for just a few seconds. Divide the dough into 4 pieces, forming each into the shape of a hot dog bun.

★ Arrange the buns on a baking sheet lined with parchment paper. Cover again, and let rise for another 30 minutes.

★ Preheat the oven to 350°F. Remove the cloth from the buns. Beat the egg yolk, and brush it over the buns. Bake for 15 to 20 minutes.

★ Poach the franks in simmering water for 10 minutes. Do not let the water boil, or the franks will burst. Drain and set aside.

★ To assemble the hot dogs: Slice a bun lengthwise, open it, and spread with 1 tablespoon homemade relish. Place a frank on the bun, and garnish with mustard and homemade ketchup. Repeat the process for the other buns.

Try sprinkling with crispy fried onions for the ultimate experience!

THE POT THICKENS

COMFORT FOOD

Alfred Hitchcock once said, "Man does not live by murder alone. He needs affection, approval, encouragement, and, occasionally, a hearty meal." I have to agree with at least the last part of his dictum, especially when I'm about to sit down to a steaming bowl of Louise Maigret's veal stew with fries!

Every now and then, a crime fighter just needs to take a break from the daily slog and enjoy a good meal, or at least tuck into a plate of real comfort food, like chicken pot pie, chili con carne, or pot roast. Not only is a little rest and relaxation good for the soul, but sometimes letting your thoughts wander while you dig into a hot meal is the best way to finally connect the dots on a stalled investigation.

BARNEY'S BEANERY TRIBUTE CHILI

BEEF AND BLACK BEAN CHILI

DIFFICULTY	EASY
PREP TIME	30 MINUTES
COOK TIME	1 HOUR 45 MINUTES
YIELD	4 SERVINGS

CASE NOTES: *Lieutenant Columbo looks at the menu in Barney's Beanery every time, but everyone knows he's going to order the usual: a comforting bowl of slow-cooked chili. There's no better prescription to clear your mind when a case has you stumped!*

INGREDIENTS

1 large onion

2 cloves garlic

1 stalk celery

21 ounces beef cheek

Salt and pepper

1 tablespoon flour

1 tablespoon ground cumin

1 teaspoon ground paprika

½ teaspoon ground pepper

2 tablespoons sunflower oil

¾ cup blonde ale

3⅓ cups beef broth, homemade (see page 115) or store bought

2 teaspoons oregano

One 28-ounce can crushed tomatoes

One 14-ounce can black beans or kidney beans

3 ounces cheddar cheese, grated

½ bunch flat-leaf parsley, chopped

Crackers, for serving

★ To prepare the aromatics for your chili: Peel and chop the onion and garlic. Dice the celery. Set aside.

★ To prepare the beef cheek: Trim away the membrane, and cut the meat into small cubes. Season to taste with salt and pepper. Set aside. In a mixing bowl, stir together the flour, cumin, paprika, and pepper.

★ Pour the sunflower oil into a Dutch oven, and warm it over medium heat. When the oil is hot, add the onion, garlic, and celery. Sauté for 2 minutes, then remove from the Dutch oven. Increase the heat to high. When the surface is smoking hot, add in the cubes of beef. Sprinkle with salt, and sear on all sides, forming a nice crust but taking care not to burn the meat.

★ Sprinkle the seared beef cubes with the flour and spices, and mix well. Deglaze the Dutch oven with the ale, and use a wooden spatula to scrape the browned bits off the bottom of the Dutch oven. Add the broth, oregano, and crushed tomatoes.

★ Stir well, adjust seasoning, and then add the beans. Cover and simmer over medium heat for at least 1 hour and 30 minutes.

★ Serve the chili in bowls, sprinkled with fresh parsley and grated cheddar cheese. Don't forget the crackers—Columbo likes to crumble them over his chili because, after all, "The crackers make the dish!"

TUESDAY NIGHT CHICKEN POT PIE

TRADITIONAL POT PIE

DIFFICULTY	EASY
PREP TIME	30 MINUTES
COOK TIME	1 HOUR
YIELD	4 SERVINGS

CASE NOTES: *The legendary Adrian Monk is very much a creature of habit, and one habit that gets him through the week is eating chicken pot pie every Tuesday night. Here's how you can make your own delicious pot pie, just like Monk!*

INGREDIENTS

1 large onion

2 carrots

3 white button mushrooms

½ bunch parsley

6 tablespoons unsalted butter, plus more for the pie pan

Salt and pepper

½ cup plus 2 tablespoons flour, plus more for the pie pan

3⅓ cups chicken broth, homemade (see page 115) or store bought

¾ cup plus 2 tablespoons whipping cream

10½ ounces rotisserie chicken, chopped or shredded

2 premade rolled pie crusts

1 egg yolk, beaten

★ Preheat the oven to 350°F. Peel and thinly slice the onion. Peel and dice the carrots. Finely chop the mushrooms. Chop the parsley. Set aside the prepared vegetables.

★ Add the butter to a large saucepan. Over medium heat, sauté the onion, carrots, and mushrooms for 5 minutes. Season with salt and pepper. Add the flour. Mix well; then pour in the chicken broth and cream while stirring continuously. While stirring, adjust seasoning as necessary, and continue to cook over low heat until the sauce thickens. Stir in the chopped parsley and chicken, and set aside.

★ Grease a pie pan with butter, and dust with flour. Line the pan with one of the pie crusts. Spoon in the filling, and cover with the second pie crust. Crimp together the edges of the crusts, to seal. Cut a vent in the center of the pie to let steam escape while baking.

★ Brush the beaten egg yolk over the pie crust, and bake for 45 to 55 minutes.

★ Serve one slice of pot pie on each plate with a side of fresh salad.

SPILL THE BEANS

SLOW-COOKED BEANS AND SAUSAGE

DIFFICULTY	EASY
PREP TIME	20 MINUTES
COOK TIME	50 MINUTES
YIELD	4 SERVINGS

CASE NOTES: *Imagine that you wanted to extract a confession from someone who couldn't tell a lie without promptly throwing up. Why not serve a hearty bowl of beans and sausage right before you ask for the truth? It would be an effective, if unconventional, approach!*

INGREDIENTS

1 bunch flat-leaf parsley

2 onions

1 stalk celery

2 cloves garlic

2 tablespoons olive oil

Salt and pepper

8 small pork sausages
(or bratwurst, or bangers)

⅔ cup white wine

5 ounces crushed tomatoes

1 tablespoon brown sugar

7 ounces canned black beans
or cannellini beans

¾ cup vegetable or beef broth,
either homemade (see pages
114–115) or store bought

4 slices rustic bread, for serving

★ Mince the parsley. Peel and finely chop the onions. Chop the celery. Use the flat side of your knife blade to smash the garlic cloves. Then set aside the prepared vegetables.

★ Pour the olive oil into a Dutch oven, and warm it over medium heat. Add the onions and celery, and sauté for 3 minutes. Sprinkle with a pinch of salt, stir, and then remove the vegetables from the Dutch oven. Turn the heat to high, add the sausages to the Dutch oven, and brown on all sides.

★ Deglaze the Dutch oven with the white wine, and then use a wooden spatula to scrape the browned bits off the bottom. Reduce heat to medium, and return the cooked vegetables to the Dutch oven. Add the smashed garlic, half the chopped parsley, the crushed tomatoes, the brown sugar, and a generous pinch of salt and pepper; stir well.

★ Rinse the beans, and add them to the stew. Pour in the broth, and then cover and simmer for 40 minutes.

★ Enjoy this rich stew with thick slices of toasted rustic bread and an ice-cold beer.

SUPPER AT THE ABBEY

GARLIC, THYME, AND ROSEMARY PORK CONFIT WITH CREAMY PARMESAN POLENTA

DIFFICULTY	EASY
PREP TIME	20 MINUTES
COOK TIME	4 TO 6 HOURS
YIELD	4 SERVINGS

CASE NOTES: *They gave you a warm welcome at the abbey, but you're not falling for it. These wise, inscrutable faces hide many secrets, and it's up to you to discover them. But there will be plenty of time for that later. Why not sit down to table with your hosts first, and feast on pork confit with broth? Surely the investigation can wait a little longer!*

INGREDIENTS

Pork

2¼ pounds boneless pork shoulder

Salt and pepper

2 tablespoons herbes de Provence

1¾ pounds onions

2 heads garlic

6 young carrots, tops removed

Olive oil, for sautéing

2 cups white wine

6 cups beef broth, homemade (see page 115) or store bought

2 bay leaves

1 teaspoon thyme

4 sprigs rosemary

Creamy Parmesan Polenta

3½ ounces Parmesan cheese

3 cups whole milk

¾ cup polenta (ground cornmeal)

2 tablespoons cream

Salt and pepper

★ Preheat the oven to 275°F. Lightly salt the meat on all sides. Sprinkle with pepper and herbes de Provence. Set aside.

★ Peel and thinly slice the onion. Halve the heads of garlic, separating the top and bottom. Peel the carrots, and slice into coins.

★ Pour a generous glug of olive oil into a Dutch oven. Warm the pot over medium heat, and then add the onions, halved heads of garlic, and carrots. Season lightly with salt and pepper; add the wine, broth, bay leaves, thyme, and rosemary. When the broth begins to simmer, add the pork.

★ Cover the Dutch oven, and bake for at least 4 hours, until the meat is falling apart.

★ When the meat is almost cooked, prepare the polenta: Grate the Parmesan, and bring the milk to a boil in a large saucepan. Season with salt, and gradually pour in the polenta. Cook over low heat, stirring continuously with a wooden spatula. Continue cooking until the polenta has thickened and begins to pull away from the edges of the saucepan. Remove the saucepan from the heat, and stir in the grated Parmesan and cream. Add a pinch of pepper and more salt, if needed.

★ Serve this dish in soup plates. Spoon polenta into the bottom of each plate, and then top with meat, vegetables, and broth.

Enjoy this dinner with a little blessing.

DINNER WITH MADDIE

EL PADRINO SPECIAL FROM EL COMPADRE:
GRILLED STEAK, BEEF TACOS, CHEESE ENCHILADAS

DIFFICULTY	MEDIUM
PREP TIME	40 MINUTES
MARINADE	30 MINUTES TO 12 HOURS
COOK TIME	1 HOUR
YIELD	4 SERVINGS

CASE NOTES: *El Compadre in Los Angeles is an institution familiar to any self-respecting Angeleno. And for Harry Bosch, it's the place to go for the best Mexican food!*

INGREDIENTS

Grilled Steak

4 small boneless ribeye steaks

1 teaspoon table salt

½ bunch fresh cilantro

2 small cloves garlic

2 teaspoons ground cumin

1 teaspoon cayenne pepper

1 teaspoon onion powder

1 teaspoon pepper

2 tablespoons tequila

Juice of 1 lime

½ cup olive oil

Cheese Enchiladas

4 tomatoes

1 red bell pepper

1 jalapeño pepper

1 yellow onion

1 clove garlic

Salt and pepper

8½ ounces cheddar cheese

3½ ounces cotija or feta cheese

6 spring onions

Drizzle of olive oil

2 tablespoons tomato paste

1 to 2 drops Tabasco® sauce

4 flour tortillas

Beef Tacos

2 shallots

1 jalapeño pepper

½ bunch parsley

12 ounces ground beef

Salt and pepper

Drizzle of olive oil

2 avocados

Juice of 1 lime

4 tablespoons salsa roja

4 taco shells

DINNER WITH MADDIE

METHOD

★ To prepare the grilled steak: Take the meat out of the refrigerator 30 minutes before cooking. Salt lightly, and set aside. Finely chop the cilantro. Smash the garlic. Add the cilantro, garlic, and all other ingredients (except the meat) to a large bowl. Stir well, then drop the meat into the resulting marinade. Cover tightly with plastic wrap, and set aside; leave it to marinate for 30 minutes at room temperature, or up to 12 hours in the refrigerator.

★ To make the cheese enchiladas: Preheat the oven to 400°F. Place the tomatoes, red bell pepper, jalapeño pepper, and onion in a baking dish. Smash and peel the garlic, and add it to the other vegetables. Season with salt and pepper. Bake for 25 minutes.

★ While the vegetables are baking, grate 1½ ounces of the cheddar; cube the rest of the cheddar and the cotija. Place the cheese cubes in a mixing bowl. Rinse the spring onions, remove the roots, and clean the stalks. Chop the onions, and add both the onions and a drizzle of olive oil to the cheese. Stir well, and set aside. Take the vegetables out of the oven. Destem the bell pepper and jalapeño, and add all the vegetables and the tomato paste to a blender. Blend to obtain a rich, flavorful enchilada sauce. Add Tabasco®, to taste. Pour half the sauce into a baking dish. One by one, fill each tortilla with the cheese cube mixture, and place it in the baking dish. Spoon the remaining sauce over the enchiladas.

★ Sprinkle with grated cheddar, and bake for 20 minutes.

★ To make the beef tacos: Peel and finely chop the shallots. Remove the seeds and membrane from the pepper, and chop the pepper. Chop half the parsley, and remove the leaves from the rest. Place the shallots, jalapeño, and chopped parsley in a mixing bowl. Add the ground beef. Season with salt and pepper, and stir well.

★ Pour a drizzle of olive oil into a frying pan, and warm over high heat. When the oil is smoking hot, add the meat mixture to the pan; cook for 2 minutes or until well browned all over, then remove from the pan and set on a paper towel.

★ Peel and remove the pits from the avocados, and then cube the flesh. Assemble the tacos: Spread salsa into each taco shell, and then fill with spicy ground beef. Spoon in some avocado, squeeze lime juice over the top, and sprinkle with parsley leaves.

★ When the cheese on the enchiladas is bubbly and the tacos are ready, it's time to cook and cut the steaks. Heat a grill or plancha over high heat. Sear the marinated steaks on all sides, and continue to cook to your desired doneness (rare or medium is preferred).

★ Transfer the steaks to a cutting board, and let the meat rest for half the cooking time. Cut into thick, juicy slices.

★ Serve with white rice and lettuce leaves, and wash it all down with a good beer—Harry's favorite is Fat Tire.

TUPPENCE'S CHOUCROUTE

ALSATIAN BEER-BRAISED SAUERKRAUT

DIFFICULTY	MEDIUM
PREP TIME	15 MINUTES
COOK TIME	2 HOURS
YIELD	4 SERVINGS

CASE NOTES: *You once dreamed of running your own private detective agency, but that doesn't seem to be in the cards anymore. Now what? Will you manage to curb your enthusiasm for investigation? You'll have to finish your soul searching later, after you enjoy the delicious-looking plate of choucroute that has just appeared on your table!*

INGREDIENTS

2 onions

9 ounces smoked pork belly

3½ ounces salt pork

6 tablespoons unsalted butter

7 ounces pork shoulder

1 teaspoon juniper berries

1 clove

2 bay leaves

1 teaspoon thyme

3 cups blonde ale

1 uncooked smoked sausage

4 frankfurters

Salt

6 yellow potatoes

★ Bring a large pot of water to a boil; add the sauerkraut, and cook for 10 minutes. Drain and rinse thoroughly with cold water; set aside.

★ Peel and thinly slice the onions. Slice the pork belly and salt pork into large rounds.

★ Melt the butter in a large Dutch oven over medium heat, and sweat the onions for 2 minutes. Add the cooked sauerkraut, pork belly, salt pork, pork shoulder, juniper berries, clove, bay leaves, and thyme. Pour in the blonde ale, and bring to a gentle boil. Cover, and cook over low heat for 1 hour and 30 minutes.

★ Add the sausages. The smoked sausage should cook for 20 minutes, and the frankfurters should cook for 10 minutes. Remove the sausages from the Dutch oven. Continue cooking the sauerkraut for another 30 minutes.

★ Bring a large pot of salted water to a boil, and drop in the potatoes (do not peel yet). Cook for 20 minutes; then drain and peel.

★ Arrange the sauerkraut, sausages, and pork on a platter. Serve with the potatoes and an ice-cold beer.

BRASSERIE DAUPHINE
BLANQUETTE DE VEAU

UPDATED VEAL STEW WITH HOMEMADE FRIES

DIFFICULTY	EASY
PREP TIME	20 MINUTES
COOK TIME	1 HOUR, 30 MINUTES (PRESSURE COOKER) OR 2 HOURS, 45 MINUTES (STOVETOP)
YIELD	4 SERVINGS

CASE NOTES: *You can really work up an appetite investigating and cross-examining. When that happens, the best thing to do is pop over to Brasserie Dauphine, right around the corner from the police station, for a nice bowl of veal stew. And since you're a regular, you can count on a plate of hot fries to go with it!*

INGREDIENTS

Veal Stew

21 ounces veal stew meat

Salt

4 large carrots

2 onions

1 stalk celery

2 leeks

2 bay leaves

1 teaspoon thyme

1 cup white wine

5 juniper berries

1 clove

8 cups water

1 teaspoon whole peppercorns

Sauce

1 cup heavy cream

Salt

3½ tablespoons unsalted butter

Heaping ⅓ cup flour

Fries

6 yellow potatoes

2 pounds beef tallow or sunflower oil

Flaky sea salt, for sprinkling

BRASSERIE DAUPHINE
BLANQUETTE DE VEAU

CASE FILE, PAGE 2

METHOD

★ To make the veal stew: Fill a Dutch oven with cold water, and immerse the meat. Bring to a boil, and poach the veal for 2 minutes, skimming off any residue from the surface of the water. Drain and rinse the pieces of veal; salt them lightly, and set aside.

★ Peel and chop the carrots, and then drop them into cold water. Peel and thinly slice the onions. Finely chop the celery. Clean the leeks, and slice the white part. Fold the green leaves around the bay leaves and thyme; then tie with string to make a bouquet garni.

★ Add all the vegetables to a pressure cooker, along with the meat, bouquet garni, white wine, juniper berries, clove, and peppercorns. Fill with water to cover.

★ Close and seal the lid of the pressure cooker. Heat on high until you just begin to hear a hissing sound. Reduce heat to medium, and cook for 1 hour and 15 minutes. (If you don't have a pressure cooker, bring the ingredients to a boil in a covered pot; then simmer for at least 2 hours and 30 minutes.)

★ When the veal is cooked, separate the broth from the other ingredients.

★ To make the sauce: Add the cream and a pinch of salt to a mixing bowl, and whisk until the cream forms relatively stiff peaks. Refrigerate until needed.

★ Melt the butter in a saucepan over medium heat. Add the flour and a pinch of salt, and stir well. Cook the flour for 2 minutes, and then pour in 1 cup of the cooking broth. Stir well, and continue adding broth until the sauce reaches your preferred texture.

★ Fold in the whipped cream, which will give the sauce a nice, airy texture. Add the vegetables and meat to the sauce, and keep warm over very low heat while you cook the fries.

★ To make the fries: Peel the potatoes. Cut them into matchsticks, and drop them into cold water. Drain the potatoes, and pat dry. In a large saucepan or deep fryer, melt the beef tallow. Heat the fat to 285°F, and drop in the potatoes to cook for 7 minutes. Transfer the fries to paper towels; set them aside while you heat the fat to 340°F. Return the fries to the fat a second time. After 5 to 7 minutes, they should be golden and soft all the way through. Transfer to paper towels.

★ Set the fries on greaseproof paper in a small basket, and sprinkle with flaky sea salt. Serve the veal stew in soup plates, dividing the meat, vegetables, and sauce evenly between them.

Bon appétit!

MIDNIGHT PAUPIETTES

VEAL PAUPIETTES WITH TOMATO SAUCE AND FRESH PEAS

DIFFICULTY	EASY
PREP TIME	20 MINUTES
COOK TIME	40 MINUTES
YIELD	4 SERVINGS

CASE NOTES: *The mystery surrounding the assault on Mathilde Stangerson is impenetrable and will require all your focus and insight. You've come up with a plan to lure the criminal out of hiding, and it involves dining one-on-one with Frédéric Larsan . . .*

INGREDIENTS

Paupiettes

18 ounces ground veal

Salt and pepper

1 clove garlic

2 shallots

1 tablespoon herbes de Provence

3 tablespoons breadcrumbs

2 tablespoons milk

1 egg

8 very thin veal escalopes or cutlets, prepared by your butcher

- -

Sauce

2 onions

2 ounces cremini mushrooms

1 stalk celery

2 carrots

Olive oil, for sautéing

1½ cup dry white wine

9 ounces crushed tomatoes

Salt and pepper

- -

11 ounces fresh peas

MIDNIGHT PAUPIETTES

CASE FILE, PAGE 2

METHOD

★ To make the paupiettes: Add the ground veal to a mixing bowl. Salt and pepper lightly. Peel and mince the garlic. Peel and finely chop the shallots. Add the garlic, shallots, herbes de Provence, breadcrumbs, milk, and egg to the mixing bowl. Thoroughly mix the ingredients to make the filling.

★ Lightly salt the escalopes on both sides, and spoon some of the filling into the center of each. Roll the sides up over the filling to form the paupiettes, and tie shut with kitchen twine. Set aside.

★ To make the sauce: Peel and finely chop the onions. Cut the stems off the mushrooms, and finely chop them. Dice the celery. Peel and dice the carrots.

★ Pour a generous drizzle of olive oil into a Dutch oven, and warm it over medium heat. Sauté the mushrooms for 2 minutes, and then add the rest of the prepped vegetables. Salt lightly, sprinkle with pepper, and then cook for another 3 to 5 minutes. Remove the vegetables from the Dutch oven.

★ Pour another drizzle of olive oil into the Dutch oven, and warm over medium heat; then place the paupiettes in the pot. Brown the paupiettes lightly on all sides, and then deglaze the pot with the white wine. Thoroughly scrape the bottom to loosen the browned bits as much as possible. Return the vegetables to the Dutch oven. Stir in the crushed tomatoes, and adjust seasoning, if necessary. Bring to a simmer, and cook for 30 minutes, covered.

★ Bring a large pot of salted water to a boil. Add the peas, and cook for 15 to 20 minutes. Drain the peas, and drop into a bowl of cold water to stop them cooking. Drain again, and set aside.

★ Serve 2 paupiettes per person with the peas and tomato sauce. Try pairing with a glass of light and fruity red wine.

PRISONER'S ROAST CHICKEN

CHICKEN WITH HERB BUTTER AND ROAST VEGETABLES

DIFFICULTY	MEDIUM
PREP TIME	20 MINUTES
COOK TIME	1 HOUR, 30 MINUTES
YIELD	4 SERVINGS

CASE NOTES: *When arrested, the infamous Arsène Lupin is held in a luxurious cell and served roast chicken with champagne. How incredible! So why such special treatment? Is it his irresistible charm? Or perhaps it has to do with a sordid affair over some invaluable Japanese stamps.*

INGREDIENTS

Herb Butter

½ bunch fresh herbs (rosemary, parsley, thyme, or other favorite)

⅔ cup unsalted butter, at room temperature, plus more for the dish

1 teaspoon flaky sea salt

8 waxy potatoes

8 young carrots

½ bunch flat-leaf parsley

1 small bulb fennel

1 whole chicken (about 3 pounds), trussed

Salt and pepper

⅔ cup chicken broth (see page 115)

Olive oil, for drizzling

8 porcini mushrooms

★ Preheat the oven to 350°F.

★ To make the herb butter: Finely chop the herbs; set aside. Cube the ⅔ cup of butter, and add it to a mixing bowl. Beat the butter with a silicone spatula, to soften. Stir in the flaky sea salt and herbs. Continue to beat the mixture until soft and creamy. Fill a piping bag (or a plastic bag with the corner cut off) with the herb butter, and set aside.

★ Peel the potatoes and carrots, and chop them into large pieces. Coarsely chop the parsley. Slice the fennel into 8 equal sections.

★ To make the chicken: Use your fingertips and the back of a soup spoon to loosen the skin from the chicken meat, taking care not to tear the skin. Insert the herb butter under the skin using the piping bag. Massage the skin with your fingertips to evenly distribute the butter all over the chicken. Set aside.

★ Grease an oven-safe dish with butter, and place the chicken in it. Arrange all the vegetables except the mushrooms around the chicken. Sprinkle with parsley. Salt and pepper the vegetables. Pour the broth into the dish, and drizzle the chicken with olive oil. Bake for 1 hour and 30 minutes, regularly basting the chicken with the cooking juices.

★ Clean the mushrooms with a damp paper towel, and quarter them. When only 15 minutes of cooking time remain, add the mushrooms to the rest of the vegetables.

★ Present the whole chicken on a platter. Serve the vegetables and cooking juices in a separate dish.

NIKU'S PASTA ALL'AMATRICIANA

SPAGHETTI WITH WHITE WINE AND GUANCIALE

DIFFICULTY	EASY
PREP TIME	15 MINUTES
COOK TIME	20 MINUTES
YIELD	4 SERVINGS

CASE NOTES: *Jessica Jones has many enemies, and few are as powerful as Kilgrave. He exercises his powers of persuasion everywhere he goes—he'll think nothing of ordering pasta all'amatriciana at a Chinese restaurant!*

INGREDIENTS

16 cherry tomatoes

Olive oil

Flaky sea salt, for sprinkling

1 yellow onion

3½ ounces guanciale (or pancetta)

4 tomatoes

2 tablespoons coarse salt

12 ounces spaghetti

⅓ cup white wine

3½ ounces Pecorino Romano cheese

Salt and pepper

★ Preheat the oven to 425°F. Arrange the cherry tomatoes on a baking sheet lined with parchment paper. Drizzle the tomatoes with olive oil, and sprinkle with a pinch of flaky sea salt. Bake for 10 to 15 minutes.

★ Peel and finely chop the onion. Cut the guanciale into small cubes. Bring a large pot of water to a boil. Core the tomatoes, and use the tip of a knife to cut an X into the skin at the base of each. Blanch the tomatoes by placing them in the boiling water for 30 seconds and then dropping them into a bowl of cold water; peel off their skins and chop them into large pieces, then set aside.

★ Pour 12 cups of water into a large pot, and add the coarse salt. Bring to a boil. Add the spaghetti, and follow the directions on the package for al dente cooking.

★ Pour a drizzle of olive oil into a large frying pan, and warm over medium heat. Cook the onion for 3 minutes or until translucent; then add the guanciale. Stir well, and cook until the fat becomes translucent; then fry for another 2 minutes. Deglaze with white wine. Stir well, and continue cooking until the wine has evaporated.

★ Add the chopped tomatoes and the oven-roasted cherry tomatoes. Season with salt and pepper, to taste. Set aside over low heat.

★ Add the al dente pasta to the sauce to finish cooking.

★ Serve immediately, sprinkled with Pecorino Romano.

RED LION
SHEPHERD'S PIE

MEAT PIE WITH MASHED POTATOES

DIFFICULTY	EASY
PREP TIME	15 MINUTES
COOK TIME	1 HOUR, 30 MINUTES
YIELD	4 SERVINGS

CASE NOTES: *Sidney Chambers is not your usual vicar: When he's not shepherding his congregation, he loves to help his friend Detective Inspector Geordie Keating solve crimes. He loves listening to jazz. And he loves going down to the local pub, the Red Lion, to eat and get drunk! This classic pub dish, washed down with a cold beer, is just the ticket when you need to clear your mind.*

INGREDIENTS

Mashed Potatoes
21 ounces yellow or fingerling potatoes
Coarse salt
¾ cup unsalted butter, very cold, plus more for the dish
¾ cup whole milk
Whole nutmeg, for grating
Flaky sea salt

- - - - - - - - - - - - - - - - -

Filling
1 onion
2 shallots
2 carrots
1 stalk celery
⅔ cup peas
½ bunch parsley
5 ounces ground beef
12 ounces ground lamb
Sunflower or other vegetable oil, for sautéing
1 tablespoon flour
½ cup red wine
1 cup veal stock
2 tablespoons Worcestershire sauce
1 tablespoon dried thyme
1 tablespoon dried rosemary
Salt and pepper

RED LION
SHEPHERD'S PIE

METHOD

★ Preheat the oven to 350°F.

★ To make the mashed potatoes: Wash but do not peel the potatoes. Place them in a large saucepan of cold water. Add 2 teaspoons of coarse salt for every 4 cups water. Bring to a boil, then cook for 20 to 25 minutes or until the potatoes are fork tender. Drain the potatoes, then peel and mash them.

★ Cube the ¾ cup of butter, and heat the milk to simmering in a saucepan.

★ Add the mashed potatoes back to the saucepan, and warm over medium heat for 2 minutes, stirring continuously with a wooden spatula, until the potatoes are dry. Remove the saucepan from the heat. Grate a little nutmeg over the mashed potatoes, and gradually fold in the cold butter. Gradually stir in the hot milk. When your mashed potatoes have a smooth, even consistency, sprinkle in a little flaky sea salt. Put the mashed potatoes into a piping bag fitted with a star tip, and set aside.

★ To make the filling: Peel and finely chop the onion and shallots. Dice the carrots and celery. Rinse the peas. Mince the parsley. Add the two types of ground meat to a bowl, season with salt, and mix to combine thoroughly.

★ Pour a drizzle of sunflower oil into a frying pan, and warm over medium heat. Add the onion, shallots, celery, and carrots to the hot oil. Season lightly with salt and pepper. Brown the vegetables for 2 to 3 minutes; then remove them from the frying pan and set aside. Increase the heat to high; when the pan is smoking hot, add the meat. Brown for 2 minutes on each side; then break up the meat using a wooden spatula. Sprinkle the meat with flour, and then deglaze the pan with the red wine and stir well. Continue to cook until the wine has evaporated.

★ Return the sautéed vegetables to the pan, along with the peas, veal stock, and Worcestershire sauce. Add the parsley, thyme, and rosemary, and stir well. Adjust seasoning, and continue to cook for 20 minutes over medium heat, covered.

★ Butter a baking dish, and spoon in the filling. Pipe the mashed potatoes over the top, and bake for 30 minutes.

Serve hot!

MRS. HUDSON'S
CHICKEN CURRY

`MARINATED CHICKEN THIGHS IN CURRY WITH BASMATI RICE`

DIFFICULTY	EASY
PREP TIME	15 MINUTES
RESTING TIME	1 TO 12 HOURS
COOK TIME	30 MINUTES
YIELD	4 SERVINGS

CASE NOTES: *Upon returning from a rough night, disheveled and with your hand sloppily bandaged, you find Watson calmly dining with Phelps. What a relief when, just a few minutes later, Mrs. Hudson has set an extra place and brought out a platter that smells deliciously of Indian spices and tea.*

INGREDIENTS

Marinade

14 ounces boneless chicken thighs

Salt

1¼ cup buttermilk

1 teaspoon curry powder

1 teaspoon garam masala

1 teaspoon turmeric

2 onions

½ head cauliflower

7 ounces fresh spinach

½ bunch fresh cilantro

2 handfuls blanched almonds

Olive oil, for sautéing

½ teaspoon curry powder

½ teaspoon garam masala

Salt and pepper

¾ cup chicken broth
(see page 115)

¼ cup whipping cream

★ First, marinate the chicken: Chop the thighs into large pieces, and place them in a mixing bowl. Salt lightly. Add the buttermilk, curry powder, garam masala, and turmeric; mix well. Cover tightly with plastic wrap, and refrigerate for at least 1 hour and up to 12 hours.

★ Peel and thinly slice the onions. Wash the cauliflower, and cut it into small florets. Chop the spinach. Mince the cilantro. Crush the almonds.

★ Warm a small Dutch oven over medium heat, and add a generous drizzle of olive oil. Sauté the onion for 5 minutes. Remove the chicken from the marinade, and cook for 5 minutes to brown.

★ Add the cauliflower and spinach. Stir in the curry powder and garam masala, and season with salt and pepper. Pour in the chicken broth. Stir to combine, bring to a simmer, and continue to cook for 12 minutes. Add the cream, cilantro, and crushed almonds. Cook for another 5 minutes before serving.

★ Serve the chicken and vegetable curry with hot basmati rice.

If your guests are still hungry, offer them a traditional Scottish breakfast of ham with fried eggs!

LAMB WITH BOURDEAU

STEWED LAMB WITH TOAST

DIFFICULTY	EASY
PREP TIME	15 MINUTES
COOK TIME	1 HOUR, 45 MINUTES
YIELD	4 SERVINGS

CASE NOTES: *For Nicolas Le Floch, lunch at the inn with Inspector Bourdeau is often a working occasion. Monsieur de Sartine demands a lot, but a good meal can help focus the mind—or at least provide a moment of delicious distraction.*

INGREDIENTS

1 large onion

4 large carrots

4 large potatoes

4 small golden ball turnips

1¼ head of cabbage

6 shiitake mushrooms

One 2-pound leg of lamb

Sunflower oil, for searing

Salt

2 bay leaves

1 teaspoon thyme

1 clove

4 juniper berries

8 cups beef broth (see page 115) or water

4 thick slices rustic bread

1 clove garlic

★ Peel and halve the onion. Broil or grill the cut sides of the onion. The blackened onion will produce a richer broth.

★ Peel the carrots, potatoes, and turnips. Chop the root vegetables and cabbage, and set aside (in water if you want to keep them from turning brown). Chop the shiitakes, and set them aside as well.

★ Place the lamb in a Dutch oven, and cover with cold water. Bring to a boil, and skim any residue off the surface; then continue boiling for 5 minutes. Drain the lamb, rinse, and pat dry. Set aside.

★ Pour a generous glug of sunflower oil into a Dutch oven, and warm it over high heat. Lightly salt the meat on all sides, and add it to the hot oil. Sear the meat on all sides; then reduce the heat to medium. To the Dutch oven with the lamb, add the blackened onion, carrots, potatoes, turnips, bay leaves, thyme, clove, and juniper berries, and pour in the beef broth or water (add a tablespoon of salt if using water). Stir well, and use a wooden spatula to scrape the browned bits from the bottom of the pot.

★ Bring to a gentle boil, cover, and continue cooking for 1 hour and 45 minutes, until the meat is very tender. When only 15 minutes of cooking time remain, add the mushrooms and cabbage.

★ Toast the bread, and rub with fresh garlic.

★ Serve the lamb with the cooking broth, the vegetables, and a side of garlic toast.

MILLER'S FISH & CHIPS

BATTERED POLLOCK WITH HOMEMADE FRIES

DIFFICULTY	EASY
PREP TIME	15 MINUTES
COOK TIME	15 TO 20 MINUTES
YIELD	4 SERVINGS

CASE NOTES: *The investigation into schoolboy Danny Latimer's murder is in full swing, and you can't afford a moment's rest. It's hard to do your job as a detective when you know the victim's family. The investigation keeps you at the office late, working with Hardy. Might as well share a nice order of fish and chips to break the ice and fill your empty bellies.*

INGREDIENTS

Batter

2 whole eggs

1⅔ cup flour

1 teaspoon salt

¾ cup plus 2 tablespoons stout beer

- -

21 ounces yellow potatoes

4 cups sunflower oil

21 ounces pollock fillets or loin

Salt and pepper

Malt vinegar, for serving

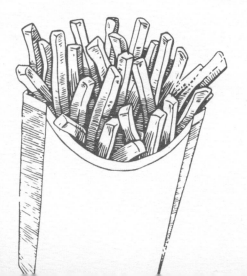

Out of the frying pan and into the fire

MILLER'S FISH & CHIPS

METHOD

★ To make the batter: Break the eggs into a mixing bowl, and beat. Pour in the flour while whisking; then add the beer and salt. Continue whisking until the batter is smooth and even. Set aside.

★ While the batter is resting, make the fries: Scrub the potatoes with a brush under a thin stream of running water. Pat dry, and cut into matchsticks. Rinse the fries in water, and pat dry again. Set aside.

★ In a deep fryer or Dutch oven, heat the sunflower oil to a temperature of 285°F (use a cooking thermometer to check). Line a large plate with paper towels.

★ Drop the fries into the hot oil for a first round of cooking. Fry for 7 minutes, then remove the fries and set them on the paper towels. Heat the oil to 340°F, then return the fries to the oil for another 5 minutes. Remove the fries from the oil, and set aside on a paper towel. Salt, to taste.

★ Finally, fry the fish: Cut the fish into large pieces of equal size, salt and pepper them lightly, and then dip the pieces in the batter. Drop the fish pieces into the very hot oil, and fry for 5 to 6 minutes; then remove the fish and set on a paper towel. If you prefer your battered fish less greasy, use additional paper towels to blot the excess oil.

★ For an authentic look, you can serve your fish and chips in newsprint paper, but either way, make sure to include a side of malt vinegar!

HUTCH'S SPECIAL

POT ROAST WITH VEGETABLES

DIFFICULTY	EASY
PREP TIME	15 MINUTES
COOK TIME	3 HOURS
YIELD	4 SERVINGS

CASE NOTES: *Starsky isn't known for his exemplary diet: He's happy to chow down on cold pizza and beer any time of the day or night. Hutch, on the other hand, is quite the chef—good enough to cook his partner's favorite roast beef, following Starsky's mother's recipe.*

INGREDIENTS

4 onions

4 carrots

6 waxy potatoes

1 zucchini

4 tomatoes

1 stalk celery

5 cloves garlic

One 3-pound beef roast

Olive oil, for sautéing

Salt and coarse ground pepper

1 cup red wine

3 cups beef broth or vegetable broth (see page 114–115)

2 bay leaves

1 teaspoon thyme

1 sprig fresh rosemary

★ Peel and cube the onions. Wash and dry the carrots and potatoes, and then cut them into large pieces. Wash the zucchini, and cut it into large sticks. Quarter the tomatoes. Halve the celery stalk. Use the palm of your hand or the flat side of a knife blade to smash the garlic cloves without removing the skin. Set aside.

★ Preheat the oven to 350°F. Warm a cast iron Dutch oven over high heat. Coat the roast with olive oil, and set it into the Dutch oven. Season evenly with salt and pepper, and sear the roast on all sides. Deglaze with the red wine. Scrape the browned bits off the bottom of the Dutch oven with a wooden spatula.

★ Reduce heat to medium, and cook for 3 minutes; then pour in the broth. Arrange the prepared vegetables around the meat, and season lightly with salt and coarse ground pepper. Add the bay leaves, thyme, and rosemary; then cover and bake for 3 hours.

★ Serve the roast and vegetables hot from the oven.

STAKEOUT CURRY

TIKKA MASALA WITH BASMATI RICE

DIFFICULTY	EASY
PREP TIME	15 MINUTES
RESTING TIME	1 TO 12 HOURS
COOK TIME	35 MINUTES
YIELD	4 SERVINGS

CASE NOTES: *The Whitechapel district is reeling from a series of horrific murders, atrocious crimes that raise the specter of the infamous Jack the Ripper. Chandler sees it as his chance to shine and advance his career, but you don't trust him—or his instincts. You've been on plenty of fruitless stakeouts, and you know what you're talking about. You wouldn't be Ray Miles otherwise. Tonight, you're having yet another tikka masala on yet another stakeout . . . Hold on . . . What was that? Did you just hear somebody scream?*

INGREDIENTS

Marinade

2 chicken breasts

Salt

2 cups plain yogurt

2 teaspoons ground paprika

1 teaspoon ground cardamom

1 teaspoon garam masala

Sauce

2 large onions

2 cloves garlic

½-inch piece fresh ginger

¼ cup olive oil

1 teaspoon paprika

1 teaspoon ground coriander

2 teaspoons garam masala

1 teaspoon table salt

½ teaspoon pepper

2 tablespoons tomato paste

3 cups tomato sauce

⅔ cup water

1 cup cream

¼ cup cashews

½ bunch fresh cilantro

¼ cup flaked almonds

1¾ cup cooked rice

★ Cut the chicken breasts into large cubes. Salt lightly, and add them to a mixing bowl. Peel and chop the ginger. Add the ginger and remaining marinade ingredients to the bowl with the chicken. Mix well, cover tightly with plastic wrap, and refrigerate for at least 1 and up to 12 hours.

★ When the chicken has finished marinating, make the sauce: Peel and chop the onions, garlic, and ginger.

★ Pour the olive oil into a Dutch oven, and warm over medium heat. Sweat the onion for 2 minutes; then add the garlic and ginger.

★ Remove the chicken from the marinade, place it in the Dutch oven, and sear it on all sides. Finally, add all the spices, salt, pepper, tomato paste, tomato sauce, and water, and stir well. Stir in the cream, and simmer for 30 minutes before adding the cashews.

★ Finely chop the cilantro. Serve the chicken tikka masala hot, with basmati rice, fresh cilantro, and flaked almonds.

JUST
DESSERTS

SNACKS & SWEETS

Baking is a form of self-expression that frees the mind, occupies the hands, and fills the stomach.

Many people feel that serving dessert adds a certain warmth to a meal. I don't know about you, but I have to agree. Eating a piece of lemon tart, banana cake, or Christmas pudding always puts a smile on my face, even if I can't recall anyone ever hiding a ruby in a cake for me.

GOLDEN COOKIES

ALMOND COOKIES WITH COCONUT AND CHOCOLATE

DIFFICULTY	EASY
PREP TIME	10 MINUTES
COOK TIME	30 MINUTES
YIELD	4 SERVINGS

CASE NOTES: *These cookies are crunchy with a soft center—rich in flavor, light in the mouth, and oh so satisfying, so . . . perfect! The cookies are so fabulous, in fact, that their creator and the prototypes went mysteriously missing. Luckily, Remington Steele was on the case, and the recipe is now safe in your hands!*

INGREDIENTS

1¾ cup plus 3 tablespoons almond flour

4 tablespoons grated coconut

1 teaspoon baking soda

Pinch of salt

¼ cup coconut oil, melted

2½ tablespoons maple syrup

1 large egg

¼ cup dark chocolate chips

½ cup blanched hazelnuts, crushed

★ Preheat the oven to 350°F. Add the almond flour, grated coconut, baking soda, and salt to a mixing bowl. Stir in the coconut oil and maple syrup. Add the egg, chocolate chips, and hazelnuts, and mix.

★ Scoop out pieces of cookie dough, and roll them into balls. Arrange the dough balls on a baking sheet lined with parchment paper. Flatten slightly, and bake for 8 to 10 minutes.

★ After baking, set the hot cookies on a wire rack to cool.

★ When the cookies are at room temperature, enjoy them right away or store them in a cookie jar for up to 4 days.

CREAM PIE FIGHT

PIE CRUST WITH CANDIED STRAWBERRIES AND WHIPPED CREAM

DIFFICULTY	MEDIUM
PREP TIME	10 MINUTES
RESTING TIME	1 HOUR
COOK TIME	45 MINUTES
YIELD	4 SERVINGS

CASE NOTES: *What better way to catch a crook at an international conference than to stage a duel—with cream pies? Clearly, David Addison and Maddie Hayes will stop at nothing to solve a crime!*

INGREDIENTS

Unsalted butter, for greasing

1 pie crust, homemade
(see page 117) or store bought

18 ounces strawberries

1 ounce fresh verbena

1¼ cup granulated sugar

Juice of 1 lemon

2 cups whipping cream, very cold

½ cup powdered sugar

★ Preheat the oven to 350°F. Grease a pie plate with butter, and line it with the pie crust. Cover the crust with a sheet of parchment paper and pie weights, and bake for 20 minutes until it is completely cooked and golden brown.

★ Clean the strawberries with a damp paper towel; then hull them, and chop into large pieces. Finely chop the verbena.

★ Add the strawberries, verbena, granulated sugar, and lemon juice to a Dutch oven. Warm over medium heat, stirring regularly. Cook for 20 minutes until the strawberries are very soft.

★ Pour the strawberry compote into a mixing bowl, and let cool for 30 minutes; then refrigerate for another 30 minutes.

★ Pour the whipping cream into a mixing bowl. Add the powdered sugar, and whisk vigorously until the cream forms stiff peaks. Fill a piping bag with the whipped cream, and set aside.

★ Pour the verbena-infused strawberry compote into the pie crust, and pipe a generous layer of whipped cream over the top.

★ Serve immediately.

BIRTHDAY CUPCAKES

LEMON MERINGUE CUPCAKES

DIFFICULTY	MEDIUM
PREP TIME	10 MINUTES
COOK TIME	30 MINUTES
YIELD	4 SERVINGS

CASE NOTES: *After all these years tracking down criminals and trying to nab Red John, your relationship with Lisbon has become . . . more intimate. She even knows a few of your most closely kept secrets, including your birthday!*

INGREDIENTS

Cupcakes

½ cup granulated sugar

4 eggs

¾ cup plus 1 tablespoon flour

2 teaspoons baking powder

½ cup plus 2 tablespoons unsalted butter, melted and cooled

Juice and zest of 1 organic lemon

Zest of 1 organic lime

Italian Meringue

3 egg whites

⅓ cup granulated sugar

Sprinkles, for decorating

Maraschino cherries, for garnishing

★ Preheat the oven to 350°F.

★ To make the cupcake batter: Add the sugar and eggs to a large bowl. Whisk until the mixture is smooth and lighter in color. Add the flour and baking powder, and stir well. Pour the melted butter into the batter, and mix in using a spatula or whisk. Add the lemon juice, lemon zest, and lime zest.

★ Spoon the batter into a muffin tin lined with paper or silicone cupcake liners, and bake for 15 minutes.

★ While the cupcakes are baking, make the Italian meringue: Add the egg whites to a mixing bowl, and beat using an electric mixer on high. When the egg whites have doubled in volume, add the sugar to a saucepan; heat to 245°F (use a cooking thermometer to check the temperature). The sugar should now be a syrup; drizzle it slowly into the egg whites while beating continuously. Keep beating the egg whites until stiff. The mixing bowl should be warm (not hot) to the touch. Put the meringue into a piping bag fitted with a star tip—or, in a pinch, you can use a plastic bag with the corner cut off.

★ After the cupcakes have cooled, pipe meringue onto each one. Decorate with sprinkles, and don't forget the candle on top!

CHRISTMAS PUDDING

PLUM PUDDING MY WAY

DIFFICULTY	EASY
PREP TIME	30 MINUTES
RESTING TIME	12 HOURS
COOK TIME	10 HOURS
YIELD	6 TO 8 SERVINGS

CASE NOTES: *Christmas pudding is a traditional British dessert that has been served on holiday tables since Victorian times. It is bursting with different flavors and textures, and it often contains symbolic objects . . . like a fabulous ruby belonging to an Egyptian prince!*

INGREDIENTS

½ cup flour

1 teaspoon ground cinnamon

⅛ teaspoon ground ginger

½ teaspoon ground nutmeg

Generous pinch of salt

¼ teaspoon baking powder

2 ounces stale rye bread

½ cup brown sugar

2 eggs

½ cup Chimay beer

⅛ cup apple cider (nonalcoholic)

1 carrot

1 cup Zante currants

⅔ cup Malaga raisins

⅔ cup golden raisins

1 cup candied orange peel

¼ cup maraschino cherries, chopped

⅓ cup dried blueberries

Zest of 1 organic orange

Beef tallow or butter, for greasing

Cognac, for the flambé

★ The night before, or up to several days before serving, prepare your pudding: Stir together the flour, cinnamon, ginger, nutmeg, salt, and baking powder in a large mixing bowl. Use a food processor to break down the stale rye into breadcrumbs, and add it to the dry ingredients along with the brown sugar. Stir well.

★ In a bowl, beat the 2 eggs. Add them to the dry ingredients, along with the beer and apple cider. Mix well, stirring by hand until the batter is smooth.

★ Finely grate the carrot, and stir into the batter, along with the candied and dried fruits and the orange zest.

★ Grease a pudding mold with beef tallow or butter, and spoon in the batter. Pat down and smooth the batter to create an even surface. Cover the mold with gauze or a cloth, and then tie string around it to secure the cloth in place.

★ Place a wire rack in the bottom of a large pot, and set the pudding mold on it. Add several inches of water to the pot, cover, and bring to a boil. Steam for 8 hours, making sure to top up the hot water regularly so that the pudding cooks evenly.

★ Remove the steamed pudding from the pot, and set aside.

★ Before serving the pudding to your guests, steam it for another 2 hours. Turn it out onto a plate, douse with the cognac, and flambé! Serve with custard.

RICK'S SMORELETTE

SWEET OMELETTE WITH MARSHMALLOWS AND CHOCOLATE

DIFFICULTY	EASY
PREP TIME	15 MINUTES
COOK TIME	10 MINUTES
YIELD	4 SERVINGS

> **CASE NOTES:** *You're one of the most respected and widely read crime novelists in New York City. Few people, however, are aware of your natural gift for creative cooking. You can't decide which you're prouder of, these smorelettes or your chocolate mousse tacos.*

INGREDIENTS

½ bar dark chocolate

8 graham crackers, broken in half

16 large marshmallows

8 eggs

4 tablespoons cream

4 teaspoons granulated sugar

1 teaspoon vanilla extract

Salt

6 tablespoons unsalted butter

★ Position the oven rack directly underneath the broiler, and preheat the oven to 425°F. Melt the chocolate in a double boiler: Chop the chocolate into pieces, and add them to a mixing bowl; then set the bowl over a pot of boiling water until the chocolate has completely melted. Remove the double boiler from the heat, but leave the mixing bowl over the hot water so that the chocolate stays melted.

★ Arrange half the graham crackers on a baking sheet lined with parchment paper. Place 2 marshmallows on each graham cracker, and bake for 2 minutes or until they start to melt. Remove the baking sheet from the oven, and top with the remaining graham crackers to make little melted marshmallow sandwiches.

★ Next, prepare 4 omelettes, one at a time: For each omelette, break 2 eggs into a mixing bowl and add 1 tablespoon cream, 1 teaspoon sugar, ¼ teaspoon vanilla, and a pinch of salt. Beat until smooth. To cook, melt 1½ tablespoons butter over medium heat, and pour the egg mixture into the pan. Cook for 2 minutes on each side. Turn off the heat. With the omelette still in the pan, pour 2 teaspoons of melted dark chocolate over one half. Set two marshmallow sandwiches on top of the chocolate. Fold the omelette over the sandwiches, and serve hot.

★ Repeat using the remaining ingredients to make 3 more smorelettes, and enjoy a decadent breakfast!

NEIGHBOR RUBEN'S BANANA BREAD

VANILLA-RUM BANANA BREAD

DIFFICULTY	EASY
PREP TIME	20 MINUTES
RESTING TIME	30 MINUTES
COOK TIME	55 MINUTES
YIELD	4 SERVINGS

CASE NOTES: *Is it because he knows how much you like rum that your neighbor added a shot of it to this banana bread? He seems to have a bit of a crush on you, although his sister would rather see you evicted. Either way, you haven't had cake this good in a very long time.*

INGREDIENTS

4 ripe bananas

2½ tablespoons unsalted butter, plus more for greasing

1½ tablespoons brown sugar, plus more for sprinkling

1 tablespoon dark rum

2 cups flour

½ cup plus 2 tablespoons almond flour

½ cup granulated sugar

2 teaspoons baking powder

½ teaspoon baking soda

3 tablespoons sunflower oil

2 tablespoons milk

½ teaspoon vanilla extract

2 eggs

★ Preheat the oven to 325°F. Use a fork to mash 2 of the bananas, then cube 1 banana, and slice 1 banana lengthwise.

★ Melt the 2½ tablespoons of butter in a frying pan over medium heat, and add the cubed and sliced bananas. Sprinkle with brown sugar, and cook for 2 minutes to caramelize, carefully stirring with a wooden spatula. When the sugar is caramelized, douse with rum; then light it carefully to flambé the bananas. Continue to cook until the rum has evaporated and the flames have died out. Set aside.

★ In a mixing bowl, combine 1¼ cups of the flour with the almond flour, brown and granulated sugars, baking powder, baking soda, and mashed bananas. Stir in the flambéed cubed bananas, and then add the oil, milk, and vanilla. Whisk vigorously until smooth.

★ Break the eggs into the batter one at a time. Stir again. Add the remaining flour, and mix well.

★ Grease the bottom of a loaf pan with butter, and pour in the batter. Arrange the flambéed sliced banana on top. Bake for 55 minutes.

★ Take the banana bread out of the oven, and let cool for 30 minutes before serving.

ROCKEFELLER PALMIERS

CINNAMON PALMIERS

DIFFICULTY	EASY
PREP TIME	15 MINUTES
COOK TIME	15 MINUTES
YIELD	4 SERVINGS

CASE NOTES: *Maurice is a famous French chef and scientist whose recipes are about to change the world. And, dear Jonathan, you are ready to fund his work . . . at least, until Maurice is murdered. Before you start tracking down his killer, it's fitting to take a moment to appreciate the last recipe Maurice ever made for you: Rockefeller palmiers.*

INGREDIENTS

Flour, for dusting

One 10-ounce puff pastry

1 egg

¼ cup brown sugar

1 teaspoon ground cinnamon

★ Preheat the oven to 350°F. Flour your work surface, and roll out the puff pastry; set aside. Beat the egg in a bowl. In a separate bowl, combine the brown sugar and cinnamon. Sprinkle ¾ of the sugar mixture over the surface of the puff pastry.

★ Starting from the left, roll the pastry from the outside toward the inside until you reach the center. Repeat the process from the right side.

★ Cut the pastry roll into ½-inch slices. Arrange the slices on a baking sheet covered with parchment paper. Flatten each slice, and brush with beaten egg. Sprinkle the remaining cinnamon and brown sugar over the top, and bake for 15 minutes.

★ When the palmiers are ready, you can serve them hot or let them cool on a wire rack.

RAN'S DOUBLE-CRUST CITRUS PIE

YUZU CREAM PIE

DIFFICULTY	MEDIUM
PREP TIME	30 MINUTES
RESTING TIME	2 HOURS
COOK TIME	40 MINUTES
YIELD	4 SERVINGS

CASE NOTES: *What wouldn't you do to win a smile from the detective who's stolen your heart? Here's how to make Shinichi Kudo's favorite dessert: lemon pie.*

INGREDIENTS

Sweet Pie Crust

4 cups flour, plus more for the work surface and pie pan

1⅓ cup powdered sugar

Zest of 1 organic lime

1 cup plus 2 tablespoons unsalted butter

2 egg yolks

1 scant cup very cold water

1 egg, for basting the crust

Yuzu Cream

1 whole egg plus 2 yolks

½ cup brown sugar

⅓ cup plus 1 tablespoon flour

2 cups whole milk

3 tablespoons yuzu juice (or lemon juice)

Zest of 1 organic yuzu (or lemon)

★ To make the pie crust: Add the 4 cups of flour and the powdered sugar to a large bowl. Stir in the lime zest. Cube the butter, and add it to the dry ingredients. Rub the butter into the flour mixture with your fingertips until it looks sandy. Mix in the egg yolks. Add the cold water all at once, and knead to form a smooth ball of dough. Cover tightly with plastic wrap, and chill for at least 2 hours in the refrigerator.

★ To make the yuzu cream: Add the whole egg and egg yolks to a mixing bowl. Add the brown sugar, and whisk together until lighter in color. Gradually pour in the flour.

★ Pour 2 tablespoons of water into a saucepan, and add the milk. Bring to a gentle boil. Whisk half the boiling milk into the egg mixture in the bowl. Pour the contents of the mixing bowl back into the remaining milk; cook over very low heat to thicken, stirring continuously with a wooden spoon. When the cream is thick, remove from heat and then stir in the yuzu or lemon juice and zest.

★ Preheat the oven to 350°F. Take your dough out of the refrigerator, and turn it out onto a floured work surface. Use a knife to cut it into 2 equal pieces. Flatten them into 2 rounds of equal size.

★ Flour a pie pan, and line it with one dough round. Press the dough firmly into the pan, and fill with yuzu cream. Cover with the second dough round, and pinch the edges of the crusts together to seal. Beat the egg, and brush it over the top crust. Make a few slits in the top of the pie to vent; then bake for 30 to 40 minutes.

★ Remove the pie from the oven, and let it cool to room temperature before serving.

Itadakimasu!

HIGH-PROOF
SOLUTIONS

COCKTAILS

Many a fate has been sealed with various potions
and concoctions—and sometimes even with cocktails!
A legendary friendship formed over creole screams
. . . a life taken by a poisoned daiquiri . . .

Still, private eyes know how to kick back and enjoy
themselves as much as the next guy. They trade
stories over a pint, they sip cocktails, and they
break out the champagne to celebrate a successful
investigation. After all, when you're a crime fighter
forced to confront humanity's basest instincts every
day, you need to know how to let off some steam.
And with experience, you'll even learn how to do it
without letting down your guard.

KING KAMEHAMEHA
BLUE HAWAIIAN

UPDATED BLUE HAWAIIAN

DIFFICULTY	EASY
PREP TIME	5 MINUTES
YIELD	1 DRINK

CASE NOTES: *This is exactly the kind of cocktail that Rick Wright might serve you at the King Kamehameha Club, where you've gone to celebrate after closing a case or playing a prank on Higgins. The simple recipe will make you feel like you're sipping a cocktail in a hammock, gazing out at the turquoise waters off Hawaii.*

INGREDIENTS

Bottom half of 1 pineapple

Juice of 1 lemon

Juice of 1 lime

⅔ ounce cane syrup

2 ounces white rum

3 ounces organic pineapple juice

1⅓ ounce coconut milk

⅔ ounce curaçao

Ice cubes, for shaking

Wooden skewers, for garnish

METHOD

★ Scoop out the flesh of the pineapple, and save the outside to use as a cup.

★ Slice or cube the pineapple flesh. Fry or grill the pineapple, and thread the pieces onto wooden skewers.

★ Add the lemon and lime juices, cane syrup, rum, pineapple juice, coconut milk, curaçao, and ice cubes to the shaker. Close and shake vigorously for 15 seconds.

★ Pour the cocktail through a strainer and into the pineapple cup. Garnish with one or two skewers of grilled pineapple, and enjoy immediately.

DEADLY DAIQUIRI

TRADITIONAL DAIQUIRI

DIFFICULTY	EASY
PREP TIME	2 MINUTES
YIELD	1 DRINK

CASE NOTES: *No one could have guessed that Heather Badcock would pay with her life for the chance to be face to face with her idol, Marina Gregg. Was it one too many daiquiris? Or a murder? Who could've had it in for the secretary of the St. John Ambulance Corps? Unless the poison wasn't meant for her . . .*

INGREDIENTS

1⅓ ounce Cuban white rum

⅔ ounce lime juice

Dash of cane syrup

1 lime round

Ice cubes, for shaking

METHOD

★ Put a martini glass in the freezer to chill. Alternatively, you can put an ice cube into the glass and remove it before pouring in the cocktail.

★ Add the rum, lime juice, syrup, and 2 large ice cubes to a shaker. Close the shaker, and shake vigorously for 30 seconds. Place the strainer over the shaker, and strain the cocktail into the glass.

★ Garnish with a lime round, and enjoy cold.

BRETT SINCLAIR'S CREOLE SCREAM

TRADITIONAL CREOLE SCREAM

DIFFICULTY	EASY
PREP TIME	5 MINUTES
YIELD	1 DRINK

CASE NOTES: *You'll never forget the day you learned to make a creole scream. The recipe was given to you by a British lord staying at the Hôtel de Paris Monte-Carlo on your first evening working there. He ended up starting a fight with an American golden boy over how many olives should be in the cocktail. The encounter between the two of them certainly set off sparks . . .*

INGREDIENTS

1⅓ ounces white rum
⅔ ounce Martini® Bianco
Dash of grenadine
Dash of lemon juice
Crushed ice
1 or 2 olives

METHOD

★ Add the rum, Martini® Bianco, grenadine, and lemon juice to a shaker. Close the shaker, and shake vigorously for 15 seconds.

★ Add crushed ice. Close again, and shake for another 5 to 8 seconds.

★ Strain the cocktail into a glass.

★ Serve with one olive . . . or two . . . or one . . . or . . . two . . .

★ ★ JOHN CONSTANTINE ★ ★
HELLBLAZER (1988–2013)

HELL TONIC

SPICY GIN AND TONIC

DIFFICULTY	EASY
PREP TIME	2 MINUTES
YIELD	1 DRINK

CASE NOTES: *When you see John Constantine walk into your pub, with a cigarette in his mouth and a smile on his lips, you know he's going to have another tangled story to tell—and that he's going to want to celebrate with one of your special gin and tonics. After all, it's his favorite drink!*

INGREDIENTS

A few ice cubes

Dash of lime juice

Dash of ginger syrup

1⅓ ounce gin (your favorite brand)

5 ounces tonic, very cold (I recommend Fever-Tree®)

1 slice lime

METHOD

★ Place a few ice cubes in a tumbler glass; then pour the lime juice, ginger syrup, and gin over the ice.

★ Mix well, and add cold tonic, to taste.

★ Garnish with a slice of lime, and serve immediately.

DETECTIVE TIPS
DOSSIER

*** HAMBURGER BUNS ***

PREP TIME	10 MINUTES
RESTING TIME	1 HOUR, 15 MINUTES
BAKE TIME	12 MINUTES
YIELD	4 BUNS

INGREDIENTS

2¾ cups all-purpose flour, plus more for dusting

1 packet (¼-ounce) active dry yeast

1½ teaspoon sugar

1½ teaspoon salt

¾ cup plus 2 tablespoons warm milk

¼ cup unsalted butter, chopped

1 egg yolk, beaten

★ Combine the 2¾ cups of flour with the yeast, salt, and sugar in a mixing bowl. Add the warm milk, and knead with your fingertips to form a smooth dough.

★ Place the mixture in the bowl of a stand mixer, and beat on a slow setting for 2 to 3 minutes. Add the butter, and beat for another 7 minutes until the dough is smooth and glossy.

★ Cover the dough with a tea towel, and let rise for 45 minutes.

★ Dust your work surface with flour. Turn out the dough, punch it down to deflate, and then separate it into 4 equal pieces. Form the dough into balls, and place the balls on a baking sheet. Cover again, and let the dough rise for another 30 minutes.

Preheat the oven to 400°F. Brush the egg yolk over the buns; then bake them for 12 minutes.

*** VEGETABLE BROTH ***

PREP TIME	10 MINUTES
COOK TIME	2 HOURS
RESTING TIME	30 MINUTES
YIELD	8 CUPS

INGREDIENTS

4 carrots	½ stalk celery
1 shallot	1 star anise
8 cups water	1 onion
1 leek, white part only	3 cardamom pods
⅔ cup white wine	

1 bouquet garni (4 parsley stems, 1 fennel stalk, 1 bay leaf, and 1 thyme sprig wrapped in the green leaves of 1 leek)

★ Cube the carrots. Peel the shallot.

★ Place all the ingredients in a stewpot, and simmer for 2 hours, covered.

★ Remove broth from heat, and let cool for 30 minutes; then strain.

*** BEEF BROTH ***

PREP TIME	20 MINUTES
COOK TIME	4 HOURS, 15 MINUTES
RESTING TIME	SEVERAL HOURS
YIELD	8 CUPS

INGREDIENTS

1 pound beef (shank or chuck)

Salt

1 clove garlic

2 carrots

2 onions

½ cup grapeseed oil

3½ tablespoons unsalted butter

8 cups water

1 bouquet garni (thyme and bay leaf tied in a green leek leaf)

1 sprig rosemary

2 juniper berries

Pinch of crushed peppercorns

★ Preheat the oven to 300°F. Cut the meat into large cubes. Salt, and set aside. Use the flat side of your knife blade to smash the garlic. Rinse and dry the carrots; do not peel them. Quarter the onions, leaving the skin on. Add the grapeseed oil and butter to a Dutch oven, and warm over medium heat. When the pot is hot, sauté the garlic, carrots, and onions.

★ Turn up the heat, and sear the meat on all sides. Pour the water into the Dutch oven, along with the bouquet garni, rosemary, juniper berries, and peppercorns. Stir well, and cover.

★ Cook in the oven for 4 hours.

★ When the broth has finished cooking, strain the contents of the Dutch oven through a layer of cheesecloth.

★ Let the broth cool to room temperature before refrigerating. After several hours, a layer of fat should form on the surface. Skim this off to de-fat your beef broth.

*** CHICKEN (OR RABBIT) BROTH ***

PREP TIME	20 MINUTES
COOK TIME	4 HOURS, 15 MINUTES
YIELD	8 CUPS

INGREDIENTS

One 4½ pound chicken or rabbit carcass

½ cup grapeseed oil

3½ tablespoons unsalted butter

1 clove garlic

2 shallots

8 cups water

1 bouquet garni (thyme and bay leaf tied in a green leek leaf)

1 sprig rosemary

2 juniper berries

Pinch of crushed peppercorns

★ Preheat the oven to 300°F. Crush the chicken or rabbit carcass, and sauté it in a stewpot with the grapeseed oil and butter. Stir, and cook over medium heat until the carcass turns golden brown. Remove the carcass from the pot, and set it aside.

★ Peel and thinly slice the garlic and shallots.

★ Skim off the fat from the cooking pot, but leave the cooking juices in place. Add the garlic and shallots, and simmer them in the cooking juices for no longer than 5 minutes over medium heat. Pour in the water, return the carcass to the pot, and add the bouquet garni.

★ Bake in the oven for 4 hours. Thirty minutes before the broth is finished, add the rosemary, juniper berries, and crushed peppercorns.

★ After 4 hours, strain the contents of the stewpot, saving only the liquid.

*** HOMEMADE MUSTARD ***

PREP TIME	30 MINUTES
RESTING TIME	48 HOURS
YIELD	1 JAR

INGREDIENTS

¼ cup yellow mustard seeds

¼ cup water

1 teaspoon salt

2½ tablespoons cider vinegar

½ teaspoon honey

½ teaspoon ground turmeric

★ Add the mustard seeds, water, and salt to a jar. Seal the jar, and leave it for 48 hours at room temperature until the mustard seeds have absorbed the brine.

★ Strain to remove excess brine. Place the brined mustard seeds in a blender, add the vinegar, and pulse for 2 minutes until the texture is creamy. Add the honey and turmeric.

★ Store the mustard in a closed jar in the refrigerator.

*** HOMEMADE KETCHUP ***

PREP TIME	30 MINUTES
COOK TIME	1 HOUR
YIELD	ONE 18-OUNCE JAR

INGREDIENTS

1 clove garlic

1 red onion

6 very ripe tomatoes

2 tablespoons olive oil

¼ teaspoon ground cumin

¼ teaspoon ground ginger

2 tablespoons tomato paste

1½ tablespoons brown sugar

½ cup red wine vinegar

Salt and freshly ground pepper

★ Peel the garlic and onion; finely chop them, and set aside. Blanch and peel the tomatoes; then chop them into large pieces, and set aside.

★ Warm the olive oil in a saucepan over medium heat. Add the garlic and onion, and sauté for 3 minutes. Sprinkle with cumin and ginger, and stir in the tomato paste. Stir well with a wooden spatula, and then add the chopped tomatoes. Mix in the brown sugar. Bring to a boil; then reduce heat to low, and cook, covered, for 45 minutes.

★ Remove the lid, and cook for an additional 10 minutes to reduce.

★ Add the red wine vinegar, salt, and pepper.

★ Use an immersion blender to blend for 2 minutes; then strain the ketchup through a piece of cheesecloth, and let cool.

★ Transfer the ketchup to an airtight container, and store it in the refrigerator for up to 10 days.

*** HOMEMADE SWEET AND SOUR PICKLES ***

PREP TIME	5 MINUTES
COOK TIME	10 MINUTES
RESTING TIME	6 HOURS
YIELD	1 JAR

INGREDIENTS

7 ounces Persian or other small cucumbers

½ cup superfine sugar

1 cup white vinegar

1½ cup water

★ Rinse and dry the cucumbers. Add them to a jar. Set aside.

★ Pour the sugar, vinegar, and water into a saucepan. Over high heat, melt the sugar and bring the mixture to a boil. Pour the hot liquid over the cucumbers, to cover.

★ Seal the jar, and leave at room temperature for 6 hours; then serve the pickles or store them in the refrigerator.

*** HOMEMADE RELISH ***

PREP TIME	10 MINUTES
RESTING TIME	12 HOURS
COOK TIME	10 MINUTES
YIELD	1 JAR

INGREDIENTS

2 cucumbers

1 stalk celery

1 onion

⅔ cup water

2 teaspoons salt

½ cup granulated sugar

½ cup cider vinegar

1 teaspoon whole-grain mustard

★ Wash and dry the cucumbers; then chop them finely. Chop the celery. Peel and dice the onion.

★ Place the cut vegetables in a mixing bowl; add the water and salt, and stir well. Cover tightly with plastic wrap, and refrigerate for 12 hours.

★ Drain the vegetable mixture, and set aside. Pour the sugar, vinegar, and mustard into a saucepan. Mix well, and turn the heat to medium. Stir in the vegetable mixture, and bring to a simmer; cook for 10 minutes.

★ Transfer the relish to a jar. Let it cool to room temperature before serving it or storing it in the refrigerator.

*** PIE CRUST ***

PREP TIME	10 MINUTES
RESTING TIME	2 HOURS
YIELD	1 CRUST

INGREDIENTS

½ cup plus 1 tablespoon unsalted butter, at room temperature

2 cups flour

½ cup plus 2 tablespoons powdered sugar

1 egg yolk

2 tablespoons cold water

Pinch of table salt

★ Chop the butter into pieces, and place it in a large bowl. Add the flour. Use your fingers to rub the butter into the flour until the mixture takes on a sandy consistency. Next, add the powdered sugar and egg yolk.

★ Knead the dough with your fingers; then add the water and salt. When the dough starts to become smooth, form it into a ball, cover it with plastic wrap, and refrigerate for at least 2 hours.

IN THE KITCHEN

★ ★ ACKNOWLEDGMENTS ★ ★

Thank you, dear reader, for reading and exploring with me all the way to the end. To everyone who has been following me from the beginning and still reads my work, thank you for your loyalty and support!

Thank you to Julien Escalas, my dear friend whose hard work and enthusiasm has made this book the beautiful, practical, and delicious thing it is. It's always a joy to work with you!

To Bérengère, thank you for sharing a life with me, for your invaluable advice, and for your unfailing love and support. Thank you for sharing your expertise on *Miss Marple*. I hope that, years from now, we'll still be rewatching old episodes of *Poirot*, no matter what else is on TV, even though we've already seen them all.

Henri, I can't wait to share all these books and movies with you. I hope you'll like them as much as I did. But just in case you don't, I'll still love you anyway.

Thank you to my parents, Bernardo and Marie-Pierre, and my sister, Laurie, for your support and love, for teaching me what it means to be passionate about something, and for always standing by me. A very special thank you to my mother, for passing on your love of reading and for teaching me how to grow and explore through books.

Thank you to my mentors and friends, Olivier, Antoine, and Julien: You add so much to my life with your friendship and your wise, valuable, and sometimes crazy advice!

Thank you to Séverine and Nicolas, whose passion and professionalism always lend a certain polish and soul to my recipes.

Thank you to everyone who contributes to making my books so beautiful.

Thank you to Catherine, Antoine, and Anne from Hachette Heroes for your faith in me over the years. It's always a joy to work with you! After more than 10 years, you would think it might be old hat, but it's not. I'm still so happy to be able to call you with my ideas and know that they'll be in good hands with you.

THIBAUD VILLANOVA
GASTRONOGEEK

INSIGHT
EDITIONS

PO Box 3088
San Rafael, CA 94912
www.insighteditions.com

Find us on Facebook: www.facebook.com/InsightEditions
Follow us on Twitter: @insighteditions
Follow us on Instagram: @insighteditions

ILLUSTRATIONS

Stamps and inlays: Julien Escalas, Dorian Bire
Shutterstock / Vecteezy: Archetype (p.12), Tofutyklein (p.12), Mamita (p.20, p.34),
MoreVector (p.52), Paintingred (p.70), Vanilin Ka (p.78)

© 2022, Hachette Livre (Hachette Pratique)
58 Rue Jean Bleuzen – 92178 Vanves Cedex France

The publisher is committed to using paper made of natural, renewable, recyclable fibers manufactured
from wood grown in sustainably managed forests. Furthermore, the publisher requires its paper
suppliers to comply with a recognized environmental certification program.

ISBN: 979-8-88663-268-2

Managing Editor: Catherine Saunier-Talec
Project Director: Antoine Béon
Project Manager: Anne Vallet
Cover and Interior Design and Production: Julien Escalas
Proofreading: Charlotte Buch-Müller
Printing: Anne-Laure Soyez
English Translation by Lisa Molle Troyer

Legal deposit: April 2022
88-7298-0/01
Printed in China by Toppan Leefung